UFOS

Are They Your Passport To Heaven
And Other Unearthly Realms?

UFOS:

ARE THEY YOUR PASSPORT TO HEAVEN

AND OTHER UNEARTHLY REALMS?

By Diane Tessman and Timothy Green Beckley

Additional research material by Sean Casteel

CONTENTS

Introduction by Timothy Green Beckley 1

The Scole Experiments—Photographing Entities, Aliens and Spirits From The Netherworld by Sean Casteel 15

The Soul, The Light and Meetings With "The One" by Sean Casteel 25

A Famous Monster Returns From The Grave by Timothy Green Beckley 33

Life After Death: We Set Sail Into The Cosmos by Diane Tessman 43

Our Cats And Dogs Do Reincarnate Back To Us! 47

What Do Heaven And UFOS Have To Do With Each Other? 53

Life—Not Death—After Life 61

    Meeting Your Maker --- 71

    When It Becomes Your Turn to Die --- 83

    Exactly Where is Heaven? --- 91

    The Highest Regions -- 97

    Visiting the Lower Regions -- 103

    Linking Up the Evidence --- 109

    Can the Dead Pick Up the Telephone and Call the Living? ---------------------- 115

    Questions Pertaining to the Subject of the Immortality of the Soul ------------ 125

    UFOs: How Do They Tie in with the Dead? ------------------------------------- 137

    Will Earth Merge with the Heavens in the New Age? ---------------------------- 149

    Electronic Transmissions from the Spirit Realms -------------------------------- 155

    The Elder Bids Us Farewell --- 168

Diane Tessman and Timothy Green Beckley

Diane Tessman is the head of the Starlite Mystic Center in St. Ansgar, Iowa, from which she publishes a variety of newsletters and publications. She is the author of *"Earth Changes Bible"* and *"Seven Rays of the Healing Millennium."* A noted channel and New Age philosopher, her work has been accredited by such authorities as Ruth Montgomery. She can be reached at Box 352, St. Ansgar, IA 50472. Readers may write for a publication list.

Timothy Green Beckley is a veteran investigator of UFOs and other unexplained phenomena. In addition to being the editor of the nationally distributed magazines, *"UFO Universe"* and *"Unsolved UFO Sightings,"* he is the president of Inner Light Publications and the author of such works as *"MJ-12 and the Riddle of Hangar 18," "Subterranean Worlds Inside Earth," "Psychic and UFO Revelations in the Last Days,"* and various other books. He can be reached in care of Inner Light Publications, Box 753, New Brunswick, NJ 08903.

A free catalog is available upon request.

UFOS – A JOURNEY TO THE AFTERLIFE
BY TIMOTHY GREEN BECKLEY

I have a secret . . . I know something you don't know.

I have made what I believe is a shocking, but monumental, discovery involving the connection between UFOs and life after death.

It is almost too strange and too bizarre to be revealed, but I must do so, as disclosing "the truth" is an essential part of the UFO "game."

Kenneth Arnold, for all intents and purposes, is regarded as the literal father of modern-day UFOlogy because on June 24, 1947, he sighted a formation of rapidly moving objects that appeared to be skipping over "water," as they moved in between the cloud-covered peaks of Mount Rainier in Washington State. Arnold was flying rather low, looking for a military plane that that was said to have gone down somewhere between Tacoma and Yakima, when his eye caught something glittering in the brilliant sunlight. "I saw the flashes were coming from a series of objects that were traveling incredibly fast. They were silvery and shiny and seemed to be shaped like a pie plate. What startled me most at this point was that I could not find any tails on them."

Arnold passed away in 1984, but his sighting has caused him to be elevated to what might be considered "saintly" status in the eyes of most UFO believers. In fact, the anniversary of Arnold's sighting is celebrated annually around the world as *"UFO Day."* Recently, I had the honor of having his granddaughter as a guest on *"Unraveling The Secrets,"* a podcast I host that is broadcast on www.PSN-Radio.com every Saturday evening. Each program is archived on YouTube and is easy to find by going to my channel, **Mr. UFO's Secret Files.**

Shanelle Schanz has an elaborate tattoo gracing her upper back, from shoulder to shoulder blade. It is a fabulous rendering showing the date of her grandfather's sighting along with an illustration of one of the objects he observed which has become etched in the memory of so many of us who take the subject of UFOs seriously. On the program, Shanelle dropped a number of bombshells, at least to the average listener not familiar with anything but Arnold's initial observance. Truth is, Arnold had a total of eight sightings of unidentified craft in his career, plus a run in with the dreaded Men-In-Black and a possible attempt by a government agent to silence him "for good."

For those not old enough to know of Kenneth Arnold's involvement in the Maury Island Incident, we suggest you grab hold of a copy of the book *"Coming of the Saucers,"* which he wrote with publisher Raymond A. Palmer in the early 1950s. It details this very disturbing case in which a UFO hovered over a boat off Maury Island, Washington, and hot molten metal fell from a large opening in the center of the craft, killing a dog and seriously injuring those onboard a small vessel parked near the harbor.

Samples of the scalding hot slag were collected and were being flown to Wright-Patterson Air Force Base in Dayton, Ohio, when the plane crashed. Two military personnel were killed when the plane exploded, some say "mysteriously."

One of those involved in the Maury Island caper, Fred Crisman, has been linked to the Kennedy assassination by New Orleans DA Jim Garrison, as popularized in Oliver Stone's cinema epic on the subject.

But this missive is about Kenneth Arnold, UFOs and matters of a supernatural nature, primary life after death and the connection between UFOs and the hereafter – if any.

Now this is where the subject at hand gets downright spooky. Creepy. Eerie. Use any assortment of adjectives you might like.

I have come to discover over the course of many years that so-called coincidences and synchronicities play a major role in the UFO phenomenon. I mean, at one time or another, we have all thought about an individual we haven't seen in ages and five minutes later the telephone will ring and it will be that same individual on the other end of the line. Hey, that's interesting but it doesn't prove much of anything.

The synchronicities in my life are much more pronounced and seem to be under the direct command of someone or "something." Some incidents that have happened to me are way beyond the pale.

What most people would refer to as a simple "coincidence" is more than just a random, chance occurrence. And, *somewhere out there, someone – or something* – is directing the "show" and trying to draw our attention to some other reality. Often these "coincidences" seem to be evidence of life after death.

For example, several years ago I was rushed to Bellevue Hospital, unable to breathe. It felt like my heart was about to explode. Because of my condition, I was taken quickly into the ER to be examined. While lying on a rather uncomfortable gurney, a series of doctors came over to me one at a time to try and diagnose my condition.

Well, believe you me, even in the Bellevue emergency room I find ways to attract a healthy dose of weirdness.

At this point, let me tell you, I was stressed out and in panic mode. Man, I couldn't catch my breath enough to walk fifty feet at this juncture. Heart racing, I saw one doctor who took my blood pressure and vital signs and spoke with me for a minute or two in order to assess my situation. She left and a young male doctor came over and asked me if I was Timothy Green. I was kind of shocked that he identified me this way and asked him how he knew my middle name since it wasn't printed on anything in connection with the hospital or my insurance. He kind of looked at me bewildered and muttered something about it being the name of a doctor he had just spoken with at the other end of the emergency room. That has to be nonsense. Absurd! Finally, he "corrected himself" and asked if I was Timothy Beckley, which was what was written on my admittance form.

What had shocked me in particular was that fact that the only person to call me Timothy Green or Timmy Green was my mom, who passed way in the late 1960s. We were rather close and shared an interest in the paranormal. In fact, our home was haunted while I was growing up, and my mother had apparently conjured up some spirits with the Ouija Board. And she had been with me when we had both seen two UFOs hovering overhead when I was ten. One seemed to be directly over our home, perhaps as a harbinger of my fascination with the subject which has lasted for well over half a century.

Thinking about the MD's use of my middle name while I was being processed into the hospital, I couldn't help but accept the fact that this was more than a mere "coincidence." It seemed obvious that this was a "sign." I heaved a sigh of relief that this was my late mother trying to tell me everything was going to be alright. I can't help but think my mom was standing nearby, stepping down from heaven, if only briefly, as I was wheeled to a private room and hooked up to all sorts of modern miracle medical contraptions that looked like they belonged at the helm of "Star Trek's" Enterprise. After three or four days of visits from my homies, who had come to wish me well, and an endless series of blood tests and examinations, a team of surgeons implanted me with an alien device. OK, it was only an earthly pacemaker, but, hey, when you're in my condition, one can feel free to fantasize, can't one?

THE JUNE 24TH ENIGMA

Now here is the kicker, the punch line, the really strange part of this and when it finally starts to come together . . .

As we have ascertained, June 24th is a very crucial day in the history of modern day UFOlogy, an accolade to when Ken Arnold had his sighting.

But what isn't generally realized is that several – no, make that numerous – UFO investigators and authors have passed away on this historic day as if the "Grim Reaper" – or someone – had hand-selected this date to usher the spirits of these famous UFOlogists from this world to the next.

I call it the June 24th Enigma!

Here is a list of those associated with the field who passed away on June 24th as best as we can determine.

FRANK SCULLY – The author of *"Behind The Flying Saucers."* This was the first bestselling book on flying saucers (circa 1950), a book that introduced the topic of crashed space ships and dead space beings to the public. Scully was a columnist for *"Variety"* and a humorist. In October and November 1949, Scully published two columns in the highly-respected show business trade publication claiming that extraterrestrial beings were recovered from a downed flying saucer near Aztec, New Mexico, based on what he said was reported to him by a scientist involved. This was long before the Roswell Incident entered the public imagination, by the way.

There were two UFO crashes, Scully claimed, one in Arizona and one in New Mexico, in a 1948 incident that involved a saucer that was nearly 100 feet (30 m) in diameter. The saucers supposedly worked on magnetic principles. In the book, Scully revealed his two sources to be Silas M. Newton and a scientist he called "Dr. Gee." Sixty-thousand copies of the book were sold. Scully was known for his idiosyncratic prose, describing Dr. Gee as having

Frank Scully passed on the seemingly prophetic date associated with Kenneth Arnold's original sighting. Scully wrote a book about UFO crashes that was a massive hit in 1950.

"more degrees than a thermometer" and an alleged crashed saucer in the Sahara as "more cracked than a psychiatrist in an auto wreck." Scully wrote another book on the subject and became the brunt of some skepticism, but he continued to show interest in the topic until his death at 72 on that "memorial" date in 1964.

Broadcaster and author Frank Edwards stands beside President Harry Truman, who it is said, was "in on" the MJ-12 panel.

FRANK EDWARDS – After WWII, the Mutual Broadcasting System hired Edwards to host a nationwide news and opinion program sponsored by the American Federation of Labor. Edwards' program was a success, and became nationally popular.

In 1948, Edwards received an advance copy of *"Flying Saucers Are Real,"* a magazine article written by retired U.S. Marine Corps Major Donald E. Keyhoe. Though already interested in the UFO reports that had earned widespread publicity since 1947, Edwards was captivated by Keyhoe's claims that the U.S. military knew the saucers were actually extraterrestrial spaceships.

Edwards began mentioning UFOs on his radio program, and wrote several books on the subject. His *"Flying Saucers: Serious Business"* is thought to have sold more copies in hardback than any other UFO book in publishing history.

He was dismissed from the radio program in 1954 for reasons that remain uncertain. His interest in UFOs was believed to be a factor, but Edwards' editor and friend, Rory Stuart, wrote:"[AFL President] George Meany insisted that Frank Edwards not mention any [competing labor union] CIO labor leaders on his program. He flatly refused and was fired." In spite of thousands of letters in protest of his dismissal, Edwards was not reinstated.

Edwards died the night before he was supposed to speak before the National UFO Conference held in Manhattan's Hotel Commodore and organized by *"Saucer News"* publisher, James W. Moseley. It turned out to be the largest UFO meeting ever held indoors, attracting a SRO audience of ten thousand over a weekend. Believers thought Edwards death to be somewhat mysterious as he was not known to be sick at the time. Edwards died June 24, 1967.

Haversack publisher Lyle Stuart (University Press) died on June 24th. He just happened to be Frank Edwards' publisher.

LYLE STUART – An even more odd twist came about when Lyle Stuart – who was the publisher of Frank Edwards' books – also died on June 24, though not the same year as his author's passing. Stuart was thought of as being pretty much of a maverick publisher, putting out controversial tomes that no one else would publish, such as an expose of Scientology. Stuart first gained national notoriety by taking on the powerful newspaper columnist Walter Winchell in a series of scathing magazine articles, collected in book form in 1953. After serving with the United States Merchant Marine and the Air Transport Command in World War II, he worked for William Randolph Hearst's International News Service, Variety, Music Business and RTW Scout.

In 1951, he launched a monthly tabloid named *"Exposé"* (name later changed to "The Independent") designed to publish those stories and articles that others wouldn't dare publish because they might offend subscribers or advertisers. Contributors included Upton Sinclair, Norman Mailer, George Seldes, Ted O. Thackrey and John Steinbeck. In another "mere coincidence," a longtime associate of mine, Harold D. Salkin, who was a supporter of many UFO contactees and groups and worked with me for many years as a UFO journalist, started out his publishing career in Lyle Stuart's office. Stuart died on June 24, 2006, at the age of 83.

JACKIE GLEASON – Actor, comedian, musician, pool hustler and paranormalist, the *"Honeymooner's"* star must have known what he was talking about when he threatened to send his TV sitcom wife "to the moon, to the moon, Alice," because he might have already been there – or close enough to see the lunar

Jackie Gleason and Richard Nixon are said to have seen an ET inside a freezer on a clandestine tour of a military hanger.

surface in a sense. As a private collector, Gleason had one of the largest libraries on psychic phenomena and UFOs. When I was 16, he sent me a letter and a check to purchase a copy of one of my earliest books, *"UFOs Around The World."* That book, as well as thousands of others from his depository on the occult, now rests in the hands of the University of Miami. Gleason lived in a circular, flying saucer-style house and was a guest from time to time on the **Long John Nebel "Party Line"** show, the first all-night radio program devoted to the strange and unexplained. Gleason also is said to have gone with golfing buddy Richard Nixon to catch a glimpse of an alien in a deep freeze stored in a secluded hanger at Homestead AFB, Florida. I remember there was supposed to be a UFO update on ABC's Nightline on June 24, 1987, to commemorate the four-decades anniversary of Arnold's encounter, but the show was presented in abbreviated form in order to add a last minute commentary about Jackie Gleason's passing that very same day.

CONGRESSMAN MARIO BIAGGI – (October 26, 1917 – June 24, 2015) was a U.S. Representative from New York (serving from 1969 to 1988) and former New York City police officer. He was elected to Congress as a Democrat from The Bronx in New York City. In 1987 and 1988, he was convicted in two separate corruption trials and resigned from Congress in 1988. He was one of the few politicians who took a serious interest in UFOs and didn't seem fazed by the possibility that he might be subject to ridicule because of his beliefs. He was an early advocate for UFO disclosure but ran afoul of the corruption laws which ended his career post haste, sans flying saucers. He died at 97 on – you guessed it – June 24th! I had once interviewed him in his office for my *"Saucers and Celebrities"* column in *"UFO Report Magazine."*

Another UFO June 24th death synchronicity which needs to be examined more fully as we search for a potential clarification.

Writer and museum curator Loren Coleman (who also happens to have Cancer as a birth sign; one day separates our birthdays in the calendar month and year) has penned a meaningful book, *"The*

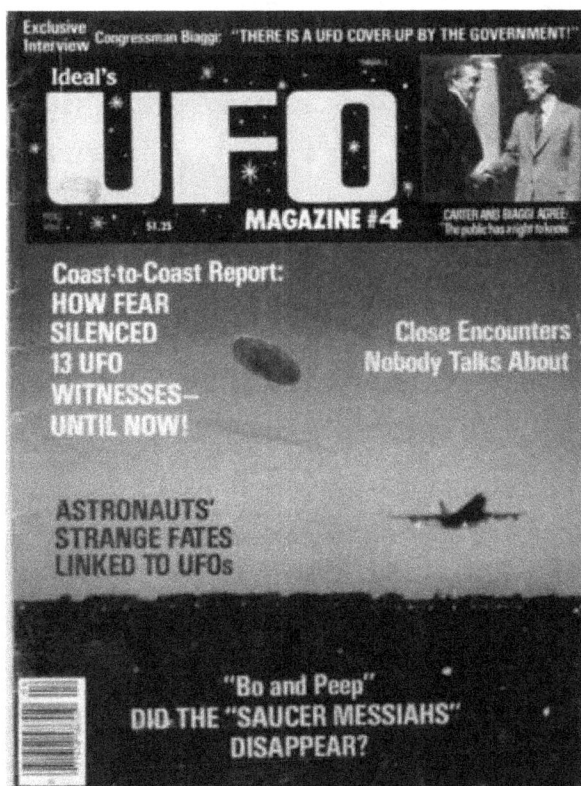

Collector's edition of "Ideal UFO Magazine" showing, in upper right corner, Mario Biaggi and President Jimmy Carter. Both were interested in the topic and perhaps they discussed the subject in private.

7

Copycat Effect: How the Media and Popular Culture Trigger the Mayhem in Tomorrow's Headlines" (Simon and Schuster). Coleman provides us with a few additional names of those who passed as part of the June 24th synchronicity.

DR. JAMES MARTIN – This esteemed Oxford-educated futurist and computer systems scientist was found floating face down in the Bermuda Triangle off his private island. In 2000, he authored a well-received book, *"After the Internet: Alien Intelligence."* In 1981, he went into business for himself as a consultant and rode the well-paid wave of consultancy for nearly thirty years. He also advised the British and American governments on computer issues, becoming the first Briton to be appointed to the US Department of Defense software scientific advisory board, and he lectured on software and systems design for over quarter of a century. He died on June 24, 2013.

Rocket scientist Willy Ley was only a half-hearted "believer" in UFOs - but he died on June 24 just the same!

WILLY LEY – Willy Ley was a German-American science writer and space advocate who helped popularize rocketry and spaceflight in both Germany and the United States. The crater Ley on the far side of the Moon is named in his honor. He was one of the first respected modern scientists who took a crack at answering the question of what is a flying saucer. He was one of the first, if not the first, persons to say that, if 85% of all sightings could be identified, what about the remaining percentage? Ley died at the age of 62 on June 24, 1969, in his home in Jackson Heights, Queens, New York.

ROBERT CHARROUX – Charroux was a pioneer of the theory of ancient astronauts, publishing at least six non-fiction works in this genre in the last decade of his life, including *"One Hundred Thousand Years of Man's Unknown History"* (1963, 1970), *"Forgotten Worlds"* (1973), *"Masters of the World"* (1974), *"The Gods Unknown"* (1974) and *"Legacy of the Gods"* (1974).* His untimely death on June 24, 1978, came as a surprise to everyone.

Of course we do not know the actual number of UFO researchers who have passed into – we hope – heavenly realms on June 24 as there is no international obituary repository for researchers of unexplained aerial phenomena. There could be many more. Your guess is as good as mine, but if you know of others who fit into this category, please drop me a line at mrufo8@hotmail.com

THE ARNOLD HYPOTHESIS

Well, if it seems we became diverted in our drive to get to the bottom of this June 24th synchronicity in which various researchers have proceeded into the great unknown, it is time we get back onto our interdimensional Route 66 and proceed to our cloud-covered destination, heaven.

For a long time, I have tried to explain to people that Arnold did NOT believe that the objects he saw on several occasions were physical ships from one or more planets. He saw them as some sort of heavenly "conveyer belt" (my term) to the other side. He didn't quite make this a secret, but I suppose no one really pressed him on his innermost thoughts concerning UFOs, and, for that matter, Arnold had a great mistrust of the press.

UFO theorist Mike Clelland has posted on his *"UFO Experience"* blog some fascinating comments about Arnold, some of which I have heard before and can confirm. Arnold's thoughts have been published here and there, but never in one place as Clelland has done.

"Arnold's experiences went well beyond that initial event in 1947," Mike notes. "Arnold went on to see a number of other UFOs throughout his life; he reported that UFOs could read his mind; he and his family saw floating orbs in their home; he claimed his phone was tapped; he was threatened by the military to keep quiet about what he knew and he was fascinated with synchronicities. He came to see these events as happening to him for a reason and he eventually saw the whole thing as a spiritual experience. Arnold also came to believe that the UFO phenomenon might represent some kind of connection between the living and the dead. All this and a pet owl on his ranch!

"Arnold had another sighting that involved a cluster of about 25 small craft. He later had yet another sighting over California in 1952. He was in his plane and flew above two distinct craft. One was 'as solid as a Chevrolet,' the other was semi-transparent, and he could look down on it from above and see the pine trees on the ground through the center of the object. He sensed these objects had the ability to change their density, seeing them as living organisms."

Here's what Kenneth Arnold said as far back as 1967: "The impression I had after observing these strange objects a second time was that they were something alive rather than machines – a living organism of some type that apparently has the ability to change its density, similar to [jelly] fish that are found in our oceans, without losing their apparent identity."

Arnold, notes Mike Clelland, had some bold ideas about UFOs in an era of nuts-and-bolts ideology. He wrote about his beliefs in the November 1962 issue of Ray Palmer's *"Flying Saucers From Other Worlds"* magazine: "After some 14 years

9

of extensive research, it is my conclusion that the so-called unidentified flying objects that have been seen in our atmosphere are not spaceships from another planet at all, but are groups and masses of living organisms that are as much a part of our atmosphere and space as the life we find in the depths of the oceans."

Below is a list of curious details in the life of Kenneth Arnold as disseminated by established conspiracy publication *"Steamshovel Press"* head honcho Kenn Thomas:

++ Initial UFO sighting in 1947

++ Another UFO sighting of two objects that he filmed

++ Another UFO sighting of 25 small craft

++ Another UFO sighting in 1952 of two objects, one solid, the other jellyfish-like

++ Arnold stated he had telepathic communication from some of these sightings

++Floating orb seen in his home

++ Fascination with synchronicities

++ Belief that UFOs were somehow connected to the dead

++ The odd details of the military transport plane from 1947

++ Government surveillance, harassment and threats

++ His investigation of the Maury Island event and meeting the mysterious Fred Crisman

++ The Maury Island event happened three days before his 1947 sighting

++ The Roswell crash purportedly took place ten days after his 1947 sighting and a pet owl! (Also noted by the late abduction researcher Budd Hopkins as a "screen memory" to hide the reality of the greys).

So, in short, Arnold believed that the UFOs he sighted were some sort of semi-living organisms, vessels that are responsible for taking the souls of the recently departed over to the other side.

Now, if this hypothesis is true, wouldn't it stand to reason that they would be personally transporting the souls who respected them and spoke so lovingly about them in life? The spirits of Frank Edwards,

Frank Scully, Jackie Gleason . . . well, we named some of them a bit earlier.

Now Arnold is not the only individual to take into consideration the possibility that these craft could be some form of "mechanical angel" of sorts.

The popular "AboveTopSecret.com" web site has posted some comments in their chat room from people attracted to this concept.

In December, 2012, *"Mandroids"* followed up on this theory that had been generating some remarks

"Could UFOs be vehicles that enable the passed on to visit our dimension? One military remote viewer spoke of seeing his deceased father aboard a UFO. Some describe the afterlife as another dimension or universe where we move to. Quantum immortality is also an interesting theory. I think this. Most departed know it and are offered brief trips to see us or our 'realm' to say hello. Perhaps transcendental beings offer this? A many-worlds tourist trip."

It didn't take long for fellow chat roomer *"Bluesma"* to chime right in about an incident involving his deceased mother.

"I must admit, I have wondered about the link between our departed and UFOs. The reason being that when I saw one in plain daylight, and quite close, hovering and then maneuvering over me while my car stalled along with everyone else's on the road, I had the sensation of being communicated with through my head. It was very strange – as if I was being communicated with telepathically. What struck me as strange is that I had the impression my mother was one of the energies doing so, and emanating from the craft. But my mother had died a couple of years before!

"I couldn't make heads or tails of how she (or her soul, or whatever) could have anything to do with a craft like I saw. It was your typical flying saucer shape, made of some sort of metallic material, and made impossible maneuvers. But it seemed very real and physical – not like lights in the air, or something vague like that, with which I would have found it easier to come to conclusions of a 'spiritual' nature.

"There were 'thought packets,' which at that time I wasn't very adept at unraveling into linear form yet, but could grasp only the general gist, which, in the case of her communications, was some sort of explanation (as I was immediately asking questions) of this being a state she 'returned' to, or otherwise went on to . . . though whether this state is actually physical (like if she was some sort of physical three dimensional entity up there) was not clear at all."

DECEASED SEEN WITH ALIENS ONBOARD UFOS

"Church of Mabus" podcast host and producer Jeffrey Pritchett expands upon this "UFOs: From here to eternity" concept in **"The National Examiner,"**

an online publication he has written for regularly. One particular article is entitled *"**Often the Dearly Deceased Are Seen With Aliens On UFOs By Contactees.**"*

"Many witnesses have confirmed having alien experiences and being inside ships and whilst doing so having seen the deceased and dearly departed. I believe on many levels aliens are also what we call angels in many scenarios throughout civilization's belief systems. This would make them the caretakers of the dead on some level if the beings being seen are in alignment with the Source of all of creation of the cosmos. Working in unison with the spiritual side of humanity to help them transition on many levels. Because often the messages conveyed are definitely messages of positivity and hope in cases like these where the recently departed are seen with these beings from the other side. So, if the contactee sees these departed loved ones with these alien beings, then it is a reassurance of life after death. Which can bring healing from grief and worry about a family member or friend who has died and passed over. I have also wondered on many levels if our spirits are in fact the same universal family as the aliens in question."

Frankly, I don't know who outside of Kenneth Arnold can claim to have latched onto this UFOs theme into the afterlife theory? I do know that Diane Tessman and I collaborated on a book "way back when."

One critic perhaps overstated the case when he proclaimed – *"'**Your Passport to Heaven'** is a nonstop thrill ride, giving its readers an insight into what it takes to ensure your passage through the pearly gates."*

Hey, who knows where we are going for sure when we die – the universe is a vast abyss I would venture to say. Being "reasonably good" should build up a bit of "Good Karma." At least I would hope so. Native shamans worldwide have long professed that they have communicated with the other side.

Many in a psychedelic state have drawn objects and beings that closely resemble UFOs and what we call "aliens." Harvard University's Dr. John Mack spent time in the Amazon conversing with the region's inhabitants and was surprised to learn that there seems to be an umbilical cord between this world and the next.

Can we get to Heaven in a UFO? Is the afterlife a lot closer than we think?

We hope you'll discover some meaningful secrets within the pages of this work of nonfiction.

Surely, Heaven awaits!

Comments And Personal Experiences Welcome

Mrufo8@hotmail.com

Mr. UFOs Secret Files channel on YouTube.com

https://www.youtube.com/user/MRUFO1100

Websites

www.ConspiracyJournal.com

www.TeslasSecretLab.com

Podcast – www.UnravelingTheSecrets.com

on www.PSN-Radio.com

Lovingly inked tattoo on the back of Kenneth Arnold's
granddaughter in tribute to his sighting of June 24, 1947.

Kenneth Arnold's granddaughter has a lot to be proud of. Shanelle Schanz holds a copy of a dossier Arnold privately self-published sometime after his history-making observation.

Arnold points at the objects he saw over Mount Ranier in Washington State.

THE SCOLE EXPERIMENTS – PHOTOGRAPHING ENTITIES, ALIENS AND SPIRITS FROM THE NETHERWORLD
BY SEAN CASTEEL

Tim Beckley has often said that he feels that what takes place inside a séance room or a haunted house is pretty much parallel to that which you can find manifesting at a UFO landing site.

"In both places," Beckley said, "you can find the levitation of objects as well as the percipient witnesses suddenly finding themselves lifting up and floating off the ground. There have also been numerous cases of people and objects passing through walls and other seemingly 'solid structures,' such as the outer hull of a UFO. When photographs are taken, eerie forms often appear on the film from 'out of nowhere,' forms that could be Ultra-terrestrials or spirit messengers."

To Beckley's way of thinking, the Scole Experiments may offer the best proof that "space beings" and spirit beings are closely aligned and have been able to show themselves under tight, rigidly controlled circumstances.

The famous Scole Experiments were a series of séances that took place in England and ran from 1993 to 1998. The experiments were conducted in the village of Scole, in the region of Norfolk, in the basement of a farmhouse that came to be called the "Scole Hole." The experiments received so much excited buzz that the prestigious Society for Psychical Research asked to observe, test and record what took place.

TECHNOLOGY MEETS THE SPIRITS

In a 2005 article, Jeff Wells called the Scole experiments "a five-year exercise in contact with discarnate entities that saw psi phenomena under exceptionally controlled circumstances. The phenomena recorded in the Scole sittings was unusually rich and obtained under protocols anticipating the objections of skeptics. There was channeling, of course, as well as spirit voices, noises, dancing

15

lights, levitations and physical manifestations of alleged spirits. Also, 'apports,' – the inexplicable materialization of dozens of objects onto the session table, including an original pristine copy of 'The Daily Mail' from January 4, 1944, and a tiny gold disc with hieroglyphics, 'the source of which has not been identified.' And remarkable captures on audio tape, photographic film and video."

Wells provides more detail on the equipment used by the experimenters.

"Photographic experiments," he writes, "included independent investigators initialing and placing unopened and unexposed film in a sealed tub, sitting with the tub at a session and then overseeing the film's development. Results included the imprinting of poetry, esoteric symbols and diagrammatic instructions to improve the transmissions.

"The video experiments began in May, 1997," Wells continues, "and were dubbed 'Project Alice' because they involved an arrangement of mirrors before a camera to capture moving images sent from the spirit world. Mirrors have long been used as an aid to receiving visions from other realms. John Dee's obsidian mirror, used by his scryer, Edward Kelley, in his Enochian work [intended to communicate with angels] is on display in the British Museum."

[Check out the Inner Light/Global Communications book *"Angel Spells: The Enochian Occult Workbook of Charms, Seals, Talismans and Ciphers,"* by various authors, including myself.]

Wells writes more of the camera experiments.

"For most of the experiments," he explains, "the camera sat on its tripod in the dark, positioned before two mirrors. At the end of the sessions, the team often saw that the camera had repeatedly and impossibly zoomed in and out on its own accord. And the tapes contained weird scenes, smiling faces, vibrant colors and hints of body parts moving across the screen in a red light. One tape showed a pink and gold line running horizontally across the screen which pivoted to reveal it was a square set on edge. As it rotated, it was seen to contain an image. According to the Scole team, 'This was a very clear view of an animated interdimensional friend, whose features, to say the least, were not exactly as our own.' They called their new friend 'Blue.' His screen capture is the classic 'gray alien.'"

MANU'S ASSESSMENT OF THE SITUATION

At this point in his article, Wells discusses an entity named "Manu," described as "a powerful and extremely spiritual guide," who had allegedly first spoken in the context of CIA-sponsored mediumistic contact experiments that began in 1952 and who also spoke to the Scole group. Manu warns of the coming of "a great awakening in many ways."

Some of the participants in the Scole "seances" as well as the writing that was said to have been made without any of the living being "responsible."

"What we do here is part of that plan," Manu declares. "There are cosmic, pulsating images coming to Earth all the time. Everything is evolving; nothing stays still. At this time in his evolution, man is ready for these energies to come upon him and give him what he is thirsting for. So we shall give him the refreshing rain of knowledge, that he may drink from these waters and that he may know of his own spiritual self.

"First, we must reach out to man's higher aspect," the spirit continues, "and then filter down to his everyday life and the choices he makes. Only that way will change come about. As you think of the people of this Earth, and the very Earth itself, so you help to activate these ancient vibrations that are coming forward at this moment. The age is right for this to happen."

According to Wells, the Scole experiments assumed that the entities with which they made contact were spirits of the dead who were curious themselves to make contact and formed a complementary team on the other side. The experimenters trusted the spirits to be who they claimed to be because of the benign nature of the contact and the fact that some channeled voices would transmit messages from loved ones containing information only the contactee could possibly know.

THE SPR REPORTS ON THE APPARENT MIRACLES

On the website of the Society for Psychical Research is more about the Scole Experiment, including some further fascinating details on the apparent "miracles" that transpired.

"There were temperature changes and breezes," writes SPR author Tom Ruffles. "Intelligent-seeming lights flashed around the room, bouncing on and seeming to go through the table, touching sitters on request and even seeming to enter them. There were patches of light forming human faces, a disembodied hand and other materializations. There were levitations of objects. Amazing images were recorded on 35 mm film: faces, glyphs, diagrams, verses, texts in various lan-

17

guages. Some 80 apports were received. The best had to be a postcard with the caption, 'If living, please write. If dead, don't bother.' Which indicates a sense of humor on someone's part."

Ruffles goes on in his cataloging of the exciting test results.

"In addition to the spectacular light shows and images," he writes, "there were thousands of hours of spirit communication. The personalities coming through were consistent,

Hands reach out across time and space — one from the living, the other manifesting, we are told, from "the other side."

sometimes answering questions before they had even been asked. Tapes in a recorder with the microphone removed still captured voices, and there were other voices which emanated from different parts of the room, referred to as an 'extended voice.' The culmination of the work was 'Project Alice,' an experiment using a video camera and mirrors angled so that it recorded its own viewfinder. The setup produced amazing images, including faces and colors, otherworldly scenes, and what seemed to be some kind of 'interdimensional doorway,' none of which could be explained by it being simple feedback or the camera's own output."

A NATIVE-AMERICAN DANCES FOR SOME SCIENTISTS

An interesting factor that argues for the authenticity of the Scole results is that many outsiders were invited to sit in on some of the sessions. In addition to the sittings in Norfolk, the group went overseas, to the Continent, Ireland and the United States. The implication is that the larger the number of sitters, the harder it would have been for fraud to occur.

As part of their reaching out to other parts of the world, the Scole team traveled to California and conducted nine separate sessions there. At one session, scientists from NASA and Stanford University were asked to attend and invited to search the room, a basement gymnasium, before the session began.

A Native American materialized during the session, dancing and chanting, and drums which were mounted high on the wall began to beat. Then familiar spirits appeared, calling some of the visiting scientists by name even though their identities were unknown by the Scole team. The spirits explained to the group that the area was an ancient sacred site and the peoples who had lived there long ago were influencing the session. Interestingly, some of the astrophysicists later started a group of their own.

THE TRULY MAGIC CRYSTAL

Back in England, one event, described as something "inexplicable by the normal laws of science," involved SPR member Arthur Ellison. A crystal, illuminated internally by the "spirit team" on the other side, levitated and settled in a Pyrex bowl. Ellison was invited to pick it up, which he did. He was then asked to try again and found that his fingers went through it. When asked for the third time, he was once more able to pick it up.

Robin Foy, one of the primary members of the original Scole team, explained that this was a metaphor for our lives, the earthly body giving way to the incorporeal, only our essence remaining when the physical is removed. Ellison was close to the bowl with his head over it to prevent a hand or mechanical device reaching in.

"It is at such points," writes Ruffles, "that these possible scenarios for fraud are stretched to their utmost."

Arthur Ellison died in 2000, two years after the Scole Experiments were concluded, so perhaps his experience with the crystal was a "metaphor" directed at him in particular?

VIOLATING LAWS OF TIME AND SPACE

Ruffles writes that the explanation for the cessation of the sittings "will play havoc with anyone's boggle threshold."

Though not proven scientifically, photographs show that levitation is possible.

"This involved entities from the future," he explains, "who were attracted to the energies being generated at Scole. Those energies were creating an 'interdimensional time wave pattern' which violated the 'cosmic and interdimensional laws relating to time and space,' thereby severing contact with the spirit team. Naturally, this brought the experiment to an abrupt end, on November 6, 1998."

It sounds a little like the spirits on the other side were "busted" for breaking a spiri-

tual law regarding time paradoxes, an idea that is complicated enough when viewed from this side of the veil but surely even more complex when one thinks of how such things are seen by whomever governs the spiritual realm. The careful "stepping around" of time paradoxes may also be a factor in UFO sightings and alien abduction since anomalies regarding time are often reported in those contexts as well.

In its report on its five-year project, the Scole group commented that, "Our understanding of what Manu [the ancient spirit mentioned earlier] told us is that humanity has, consciously or unconsciously, been sending out a signal asking for help for our world for some time and that many loving beings have heard our plea. They are now coming in response to our request to aid us in any way they possibly can. It seems that many dimensions are bound together with the common thread of love. This love transcends all other things. What a truly wonderful notion that is."

WHITLEY STRIEBER COMMENTS ON THE SCOLE EXPERIMENTS

When I interviewed alien abductee and bestselling author Whitley Strieber in 2012, I asked him about the Scole Experiments and the image capture of an entity identical to the gray aliens so often seen in ET encounters.

"The image that was seen in the Scole Experiments was very interesting to me," Strieber replied, "because I think that whatever is here has come into contact with that level of human being first, that they are already well-involved with what we call the dead and are just now beginning to penetrate deeper into the body of the species, into the more dense areas, which is where we are, the living. The more dense physical area.

"And I'm not so sure," he continued, "that they have the ability to completely express themselves in the physical realm. I suspect that part of their interest in us might be that we have these two very distinct levels of being. We're like the caterpillars and the dead are the butterflies. But I wouldn't say, for example, that the dead are a supernatural element at all. I think they're part of the physical world, but a part of it that we don't understand or know how to address yet. So I found that picture [the gray alien image capture] very interesting and very supportive of what our findings are."

STRIEBER'S VISITATIONS FROM THE DEAD

I also asked Strieber about the appearance of deceased friends and family sometimes reported by close encounter experiencers.

"I have been thinking a lot about that," he answered, "because there can be no question that this is true. It has appeared in so many of the letters that we've

Whitley Strieber (left) and Sean Casteel (right) at the Dark Delicacies bookstore in Burbank, California.

received, in my own life, and in experiences that groups of people have had in our cabin in upstate New York. So it is true. When I had my first close encounter, there was a man there who I knew. And I was astonished to find a few weeks after my experience, the December of 1985 experience, that he'd been dead since the previous March. The reason I initially thought that I was the victim of some kind of criminal activity, being assaulted and drugged and so forth, was that he was there. He had been a Central Intelligence Agency agent and I was just suspicious that something was up. I didn't know quite what it would be, but I was very suspicious. Then I was amazed to find out that he was dead. I've even seen his grave. He's certainly dead.

"We used to have people in groups up to our cabin," Strieber went on, "and we found that they often would see the dead in the context of the Visitors [Strieber's name for the aliens]. Two people sleeping in the bed in the basement woke up to find a dead friend standing at the foot of the bed. In the letters we've received, it's absolutely commonplace. So I've discarded the idea that this is 'scientists from another planet' coming here to study us. It's something else. I think that what it represents in part – and it's very complicated – is mankind's next step, our movement to another level of being in which what we call the dead will not be so mysterious. They will be part of life in a certain way. I think that the Visitors bring with them – and understand, I don't say that I think they're not aliens. I don't know what they are. But they bring with them a dropping of the veil between the living and the dead."

I reminded Strieber at that point that he had once said something about the dead coming to dwell among us, the living.

"Well, I don't know why they wouldn't be," he said. "I have had in my experience a relationship with someone I regarded – and who identified himself – as dead. The relationship lasted for three years. He had a limited ability to manifest a physical presence. When he was physical, he was very small and very light, but definitely human-feeling and looking. The very last time that I would ever see him, at that cabin in upstate New York, he manifested as a glowing light and it was absolutely awesome. He indicated to me during the course of our relationship that he was from 'between the lives,' that he would eventually one day be in the physical again.

"Interestingly enough," Strieber said, "his primary concern, when he first showed up in my life, was the degree of my loyalty to my wife. And that was tested. The other thing that happened first, before he proceeded, was a 'life review' where he went through my life with me and did it in my mind in pictures. Incident after incident after incident of my life, looking for where my conscience resided. Once I seemed to have passed these tests, then the relationship grew."

Even those with only a cursory knowledge of Near-Death-Experiences will recognize the familiar "life review" phase that often takes place after the soul has been ushered into the presence of the great and loving light. Strieber's remarks in the interview also touch on spiritualism as he describes befriending an only partially physically-manifested soul who told him he was "between the lives," which seems to mean Strieber's friend was awaiting reincarnation and beginning life anew. The occupants of the UFOs and the residents of the spirit world manifest themselves in so many ways and in so many lives but rarely do so as clearly as in the life of Whitley Strieber.

SUGGESTED READING

"The Scole Experiment" by Grant and Jane Solomon

"Solving The Communion Enigma," by Whitley Strieber

FOR VIEWING ON YOUTUBE OR ON DVD BY UFOTV:

"The After Life Investigations"

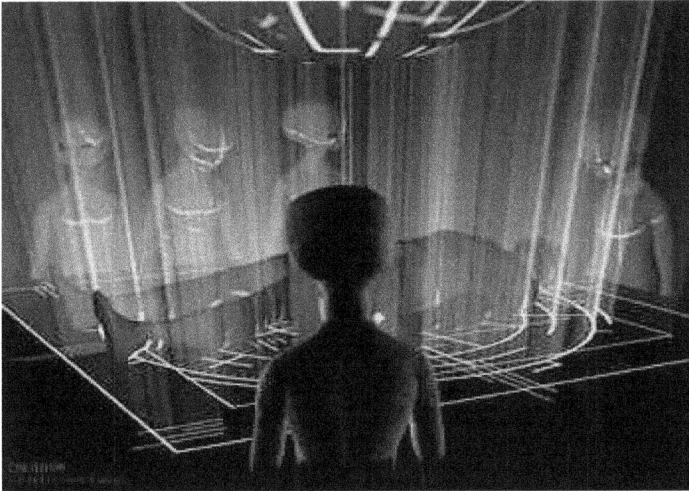

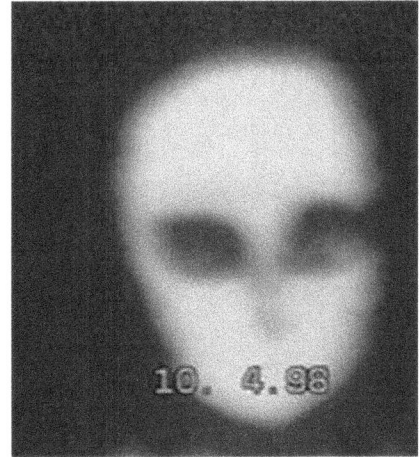

ET-looking beings began to appear on the film among the many
unusual photographic images.

Strange pyramid shapes also rendered themselves visible – a link
perhaps to the afterlife or another world?

The "spirits" seem to indicate through
photographic images that
they may not be from this world but
from somewhere deep in space.

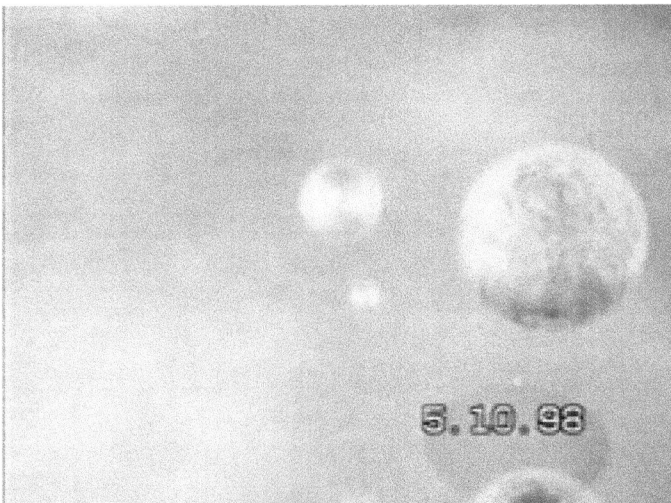

Figure 53. Betty is greeted by an Elder as she steps out of the blue machine.

It's gettin' dark, too dark for me to see
I feel like I'm knockin' on heaven's door.

- Bob Dylan

THE SOUL, THE LIGHT AND MEETINGS WITH "THE ONE"
BY SEAN CASTEEL

The primary authors of this book, Tim and Diane, want readers to realize that there is a direct link between what parapsychologists term the Near Death Experience (NDE) and the experiences of UFO abductees and contactees.

The heavenly realm that all of us hope to reach upon our departure from this life seems to be populated by energy forms of all types of "the Other," be they aliens, spirits or those forms who are said to wander about the astral plane.

Now, this concept may be relatively new to us, but native shamans from all over the world have revered this heavenly netherworld since ancient man first started peering into the void – with and without the use of ceremonial "stimulants." The late Harvard psychiatrist, Dr. John Mack, spent time among native peoples in the Amazon region and explored these spirit/alien connections with great interest in the years before his tragic passing.

This chapter offers the experiences of some UFO abductees who have crossed over into zones of bliss and healing that one does not automatically assume will come with the territory when one is dealing with flying saucers and their occupants.

A DEVOUT CHRISTIAN ABDUCTEE MEETS "THE ONE"

Betty Andreasson Luca is another lifelong abductee whose experiences also echo the Near-Death Experience. An article by Joseph Kerrick summarizes some of Betty's experiences as reported in UFO researcher Raymond E. Fowler's series of books on Betty that began with "*The Andreasson Affair,*" which was first published in 1979 and was followed by several sequels.

Under hypnosis, Betty recalled being taken to visit "the One," which is instantly recognizable as the same type of experience reported by many Near-Death-Experiencers and might even be called an "identical" experience, according to Kerrick.

Betty Andreasson Luca

"It is a very basic kind of spiritual experience," Kerrick writes, "which has also been consistently reported throughout history by saints, mystics and various types of ecstatics."

Kerrick is quick to point out that the similarities between UFO abductions and NDEs have been explored most famously by Dr. Kenneth Ring, a psychologist and professor at the University of Connecticut who has published several important books on the subject, to include *"Life At Death," "Heading Toward Omega" and "The Omega Project: Near-Death Experiences, UFO Encounters, and Mind at Large."* There will be more from Dr. Ring later in this chapter.

Along with Dr. Ring, writer and researcher Dr. Brenda Denzler is also a source Kerrick draws on to give some background for this approach to "heavenly" UFO occupants.

"According to polls," Denzler writes, "we live in an age where now most believe that UFOs are real and that 'people like us live on other planets.' In that context, since angels and demons are out of style, they now dress in the costume of our own epoch's archetypal figure – the extraterrestrial alien – whom we can see precisely because we can now CONCEIVE of him; he conforms to and expresses our current ideas of possibility.

"Abductions may represent a contemporary form of the shamanic journey," she continues, "one that fits and is phrased in terms of a highly technological society which has already turned its imaginative attention to star flight. Indeed, in an age where secular thinking has come to be the standard but from which the religious impulse has never disappeared, it is psychologically very understandable why traditional religious images of salvation have come to be projected onto the screen of a universe where, for some, it is easier to believe in ETs than in God."

Betty does believe in God very strongly and is a devout Christian. But there is an important difference between her experiences and that of NDEr's. She was escorted to her audience with the radiant, loving light called "the One" not by dead relatives nor Christian spiritual figures but by small, gray, bug-eyed space aliens. Her first such ecstatic encounter took place when she was only 13 years old and was recalled under hypnosis much later in her life. Along with the grays, there appeared entities who were human-looking except for their size, being about seven feet tall; they were dressed in long white robes, had pale-colored skin, and hair that was blonde to white.

"In a word, they looked exactly like the Christian image of angels," Kerrick writes, "except that they had no wings. Betty called these beings 'the Elders,' after the Christian term used in the Book of Revelation denoting the angelic beings surrounding the throne of God."

A BLESSING FROM THE ELDERS

As reported in Ray Fowler's book, *"The Watchers II,"* the small grays came for Betty in a saucer and took her into outer space, where the small craft docked with a huge cylindrical mothership. This was the domain of the Elders, who apparently commanded the grays in a symbiotic relationship. Betty asked why she was there with the Elders and they said, "Don't you remember your blessing?"

She didn't know what they were talking about, so in response they used a machine to show her a scene from earlier in her life.

"It was at a church service," Kerrick explains, "and what happened was this: Betty stood up and gave testimony and pledged to use her talents for the glory of God. This was probably not unusual for this type of service. But then the minister suddenly began speaking in tongues. His wife jumped up, ran down the aisle to Betty, put her hands on Betty's head and began speaking in tongues herself. Then the minister interpreted his wife's tongues; it was a message for Betty: 'You have given all that you have . . . thou shalt be blessed above women.'"

That was the scene as Betty remembered it from her youth. But now, in the strange replay on the mothership, she noticed some differences.

"Some of the people had 'a light around them,'" Kerrick writes. "These included Betty, the minister and his wife. And two Elders were present in the room, unseen by the congregation. One of the Elders stood behind the minister and put his hand on the man's shoulder – and this is when he began speaking in tongues. Then the other Elder whispered in the ear of the minister's wife, and this is when she jumped up and administered the 'blessing' to Betty. Evidently, the whole scenario had been orchestrated by the Elders."

When Betty asked the Elders who they were, they replied that they are "the ambassadors of Oh, masters of rings, cycles and orbs." Who is Oh? Betty asked. "Oh is the internal, external, eternal presence," an Elder replied.

THE STRUGGLE FOR A SOUL

Next, Betty was startled to have another out-of-body experience. She emerged in her "subtle" body and was led through a portal made of rippling waves of energy. At one point during this experience, the Elder touched Betty's shoulder, which was followed by a little explosion of light. They were now in a different place, a hospital room where a very old man lay in a bed while a nurse watched over him.

"And there was more," Kerrick writes. "Two small entities which seemed to be made of darkness were tugging at the man, as if trying to pull his soul out of his body – this was Betty's impression. But there was also present a light being; this was the type of entity Betty had encountered before in her experiences. It had no visible human features but appeared as a bodily form made of white light. This being was also tugging at the dying man; it was clearly a battle for his soul between these opposing entities. The Elder resolved the conflict: he threw two tiny balls of light at the black entities, and they flew away."

The Elder and Betty next traveled to a woods where a small saucer and two of the grays awaited them. As they flew into the sky, Betty asked where they were going now and was told they were going to see the One. The craft came to a stop and they emerged into a place filled with bright light. Above them was the Great Door, which was the source of the light. The Elder touched one of the grays on the shoulder and spoke to him. The gray came along with the Elder and Betty as they walked toward the light. The small group began to run, hastening to move into the pure radiance. Betty was overwhelmed with the ecstasy of the One, which she re-experienced on the hypnotist's couch. Several people in attendance during the hypnosis session were all profoundly moved by the visible effects of her transformation.

"Betty, the Elder and the gray all turned into light beings as they went into the One," Kerrick recounts. "Each was a different hue: the Elder's light-body was pure white, the gray alien's was light blue, and Betty's was golden. Betty said, 'Oh, there is such love . . . Oh, there is such peace . . . I'm just engulfed in light and blending into that light. Oh, this is everything, everything, everything. I cannot explain the wonder and beauty and love and peace.' And then a heartbroken cry as Betty realized that she would have to leave this beatific state of Oneness. 'Oh, I'm going to have to go back. I have to go back for others so that they too will see, will understand and know.'"

At that point, Betty, the Elder and the gray emerged back out of the light and turned back into their normal forms. Betty was escorted back into the saucer and taken home by the grays. She found her physical body sitting up on the side of her bed next to her sleeping husband and re-entered it. The experience had ended.

RAYMOND FOWLER AND THE WATCHERS

Of course, all of Betty's spiritual adventures were not lost on Raymond

Raymond Fowler

Fowler, the veteran UFO researcher who investigated her case over a series of landmark books on alien abduction. In an online interview with Dan Boudillion, Ray was asked if he felt his own abduction experiences were linked with Betty's at some deeper level.

"I don't know," Ray replied. "I do know that I was attracted to her case not only because Dr. J. Allen Hynek [an early investigator of UFOs who worked for the Air Force] referred me to it but also because she is a Christian. Initially, I was interested in how a Christian would process an abduction experience. Also, and importantly, it was my exposure to her childhood contact and abduction experiences that once again triggered memories of my own similar childhood experiences and my future exploration of them."

Ray told Boudillion that he and Betty had once received the typical scoop marks left behind after an abduction during the same week and were told by the entities that they were going to do something important for mankind.

"Regarding the latter," Ray said, "other than my books and investigation reports, I have not done anything earthshaking for mankind."

Focusing on the subject at hand, Ray commented on the fact that some NDEs and UFO experiences would be hard to tell apart. Like many who speak on this relationship, Ray mentioned the research of Dr. Kenneth Ring, who has stated that some persons who have had an NDE report being in a craft in outer space and being confronted with entities similar to the robed, humanlike Elders experienced by Betty and Ray himself.

"Similar entities are reported," Ray said, "in normal NDEs and in ancient and modern so-called religious experiences. This being the case, one could speculate that UFOs and the entities that operate them come from that same domain/dimension that persons having a NDE enter and return from. In 'The Andreasson Legacy,' I speculate that human beings are a larval form of the so-called Elders and we, like a herd of cattle, are being cared for and maintained until we die and enter the reality in which they dwell."

Such beliefs were not always a part of Ray's spiritual perspective.

"At one time," he explained, "I was a fundamentalist Christian but since have expanded my theology. I had dismissed anything paranormal experienced by myself or my family as being Satanic. In my early days as a UFO investigator, I rejected any UFO report that contained any type of psychic phenomena. I also felt that UFO witnesses who reported such were mentally unstable. However, it became apparent that credible persons were reporting incredible things that were similar to what my family, especially my father, had and were experiencing. My mind and theology gradually broadened to accept the paranormal aspects of the UFO phenomenon."

When asked by Boudillion what was the most important message or insight he'd like to pass on after a lifetime of UFO research, Ray answered, "That UFOs, NDEs and so-called psychic phenomena are individual expressions of an all-encompassing meta-phenomenon that is generated from another reality into our world, which is but a shadowy reflection of that other reality."

DR. KENNETH RING REPORTS A HEALING

Dr. Kenneth Ring is the most-referred-to expert I encountered while researching the connection between UFO abduction and NDEs. But the relationship between the two phenomena was not always apparent even to him.

In his 1992 book, *"The Omega Project,"* he writes, "Our survey of the various major facets of NDEs has shown repeatedly how they represent, on almost every point of comparison, the polar opposite of CE IVs [Close Encounters of the Fourth Kind, or abduction experiences]. Not only is the content of the two experiences vastly different, to say nothing of the emotional response to them, but the very qualities of these two categories of extraordinary encounters also stand in blatant contrast to each other. NDEs are subjectively highly real, even in their transcendental aspects, whereas UFO alien encounters have a curious dreamlike or even fantastic flavor. The worlds that they open to their respective travelers seem, perhaps quite literally and not just metaphorically, to reside in altogether different universes.

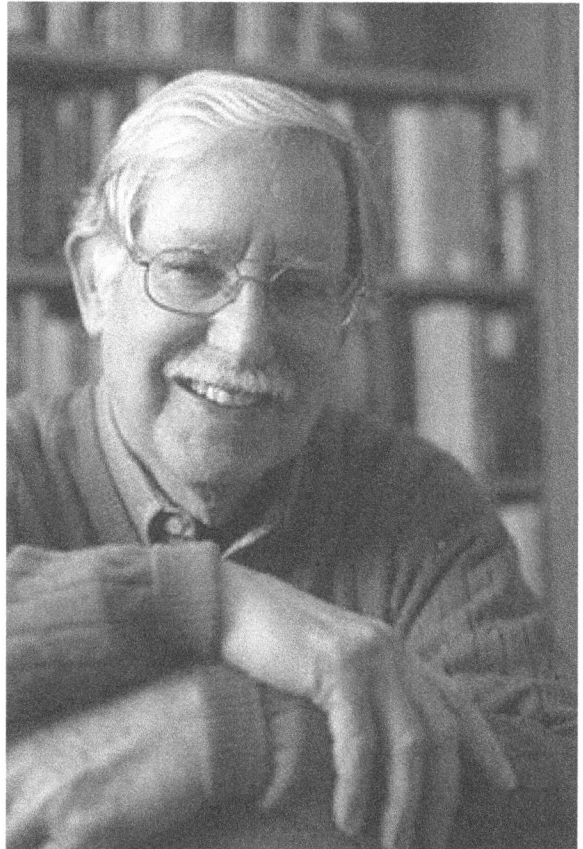

"That much, at least, seems obvious," Ring continues. "And yet, what is obvious may not be true. As a case in point, consider the following narrative. When you read it, please decide into which of our two categories it should be placed."

Ring next begins to tell the story of Beryl Hendricks, a thirty-nine-year-old college-educated woman who operates a day care center in New York State. In 1977, she had a benign tumor removed from her breast, but in the early summer of the next year, she discovered another one "about the size of a golf ball." Intending to call her physician the next day, she remembers going downstairs that night to be with her husband on the couch. Beryl has no recollection of passing out, but her husband was there and does remember it. He took her pulse and found she didn't have one, which he told her later.

Meanwhile, Beryl had entered a non-ordinary reality, according to Ring.

"The next thing I remember was looking out of a round window," she said, "and seeing the blackest blackness with tiny white sparkles. I later realized I was experiencing deep space. I felt cold, colder than I have ever experienced. I was unconcerned about my predicament and I turned my gaze from the window. There was a bright white light directly above me with four to seven thin, tall figures around me. I later realized I was on some kind of operating table. I was given two messages telepathically."

The first message was "Look and see – it is gone."

The second message was "Follow your husband." (Beryl and her husband had been experiencing marital difficulty at the time.)

"All of a sudden," she recalled, "I was tumbling head over heels (figuratively, as I was out of my body) and saw the earth as geometric green and was shown land masses, changing, getting closer and closer, not unlike an airplane crashing, traveling at unbelievable speed, and finally falling from the couch to the floor; vomiting relentlessly.

"Two hours passed," Beryl went on, "and when I washed the vomit off, the lump was gone – totally. In the ten years since this experience, my health has been excellent and I have, with my husband, found a close personal relationship with God."

In responding to Beryl's story, Ring asks the reader, "What on earth – or in heaven – do we have here? Is this an NDE or some kind of UFO encounter? Clearly, it has elements of both, and just as clearly it threatens to confound our neat dichotomy between these two types of experience."

Ring informs us that he calls this sort of case a "mixed motif" and that there are several in his files.

"Among my respondents, I have found others who, in describing what purports to be an NDE, begin to talk about UFOs and aliens in the same context. Furthermore, there turns out to be a small but respectable number of persons in my sample who report having had, at different times, both an NDE and one or more UFO encounters."

Could it be, Ring asks, that the world of the NDE and that of the UFO abduction, for all their differences, are not, after all, universes apart, but a part of the SAME universe? And, second, could it be that NDErs and UFO experiencers have more in common with one another than we have heretofore suspected?

It is the hope of the authors of this book that the answer to both of Ring's questions is a reassuringly resounding YES!

SUGGESTED READING

"Heading Toward Omega," by Dr. Kenneth Ring

"The Omega Project: Near Death Experiences, UFO Encounters and Mind At Large," by Dr. Kenneth Ring

"The Andreasson Legacy," by Raymond Fowler

"UFO Testament: Anatomy of an Abductee," by Raymond Fowler

"The Heretic's UFO Guidebook," by Sean Casteel.

"Angel Spells: The Enochian Occult Workbook of Charms, Seals, Talismans and Ciphers," by various authors, including Tim Beckley and Sean Casteel

Artwork rendered under the influence of ayahuasca

A FAMOUS MONSTER RETURNS FROM THE GRAVE
BY TIMOTHY GREEN BECKLEY

I wish to tell a story of what is, to me at least, an incident which greatly bolsters the authors' case for the possibility – if not the likelihood – that there is somehow a connection between our loved ones on the other side and our friends "from on high." I hesitate to refer to the higher ones as aliens, as my coauthor Diane is more prone to do because of her lifelong experiences with them. I have adopted the term "Ultra-terrestrial" to best describe these beings or entities or pure energies that seem to coexist or easily mingle with those of us here in what we call the material world. And so I begin.

Anyone over the age of 50 will immediately recognize the name of Forest J. Ackerman, especially if you were a young boy living in the late fifties, sixties and seventies.

For a period of nearly five decades, *"Famous Monsters of Filmland"* dominated the pulp magazine racks in newsstands throughout America. Under the editorial helm of "Uncle Forry," as he was best known by a multitude of followers, "FM" offered brief articles, well-illustrated with publicity stills and graphic artwork, on horror movies from the silent era to the then-present, their stars and filmmakers. The publication was specifically aimed at late pre-adolescents and young teenagers who couldn't get enough of Dracula, Frankenstein and all the other ghouls and ghosties that went bump in the night – all the nightmarish creatures that had been popularized on the big screen and were now invading our homes through the advent of the invention of something called television.

Not surprisingly, the content of the magazine influenced many would-be, hopeful filmmakers who would later emblazon their own mark on Hollywood, including the likes of Steven Spielberg, who once wrote to the magazine and had his photo published as a teenager. In his 2000 nonfiction book, *"On Writing,"* Stephen King recounts his own history with Ackerman's work and calls *"Famous*

33

Monsters of Filmland" a "life-changing" publication, adding: "Ask anyone who has been associated with the fantasy–horror–science fiction genres in the last thirty years about this magazine and you'll get a laugh, a flash of the eyes, and a stream of bright memories – I practically guarantee it."

And, of course, I was reading *"Famous Monsters"* along with all my contemporaries!

In the wings, waiting for a chance at becoming a seasoned cinema mogul himself, was a highly motivated Paul Jeffrey Davids, who grew up in Kensington and Bethesda, Maryland, the son of Dr. Jules Davids (Ph.D.), the late tenured full-professor of American Diplomatic History at Georgetown University in Georgetown's School of Foreign Service. Becoming a winner in the first *"Famous Monsters of Filmland's"* Amateur Movie Contest at age fourteen was an early influence for Paul Davids in choosing a career in motion picture production. From his elementary school days onward, he made many amateur science fiction, dinosaur, dragon and monster films using stop-motion animation, and his cinematic heroes from a young age were Ray Harryhausen, George Pal and, naturally, Forrest J Ackerman.

Though he had worked on other productions in Hollywood both for the big screen and for television, his first stellar break came when Marvel Productions hired him as the production coordinator for *"The Transformers"* animated series. His career blossomed after this, even though he had already established himself a writer for the *"Star Wars"* novel series.

I first met Paul around the time he was wrapping on his first major motion picture. *"Roswell"* was initially supposed to be a Home Box Office release, but HBO fumbled the ball and Davids eventually found a new home for the highly anticipated production with Showtime. The movie is now regarded by many Roswell aficionados as a major opus – adding respectable support to their belief that the incident really took place and that a space vehicle from another planet, complete with alien visitors, actually crashed in the New Mexican desert. The look and feel of the film had viewers believing they were actually back on the Army Air Base at the time of the supposed UFO crash in 1947, as well as at several reunions of the military personnel who were stationed there.

I'm sure Paul doesn't want the public to think that he is capable of excelling only in the sci-fi genre because he has pretty much adapted to the overall Hollywood scheme of things, having produced films like *"Jesus in India,"* *"Timothy Leary's Dead,"* *"Starry Nights,"* about Vincent Van Gogh, and, most recently, *"The Life After Death Project"* – which is where our story really begins to take shape, if only in ectoplasmic form.

In 2014, I decided that it was about time to start my own YouTube channel. I had traveled far and wide around the 50 States setting up my tripod and chatting with some of the luminaries in the paranormal and Fortean fields. I taped the shows and would transfer them to DVD and give them out to those who purchased books from our website and through the mail at The Conspiracy Journal/Inner light Publications.

The interviews are not of a Hollywood variety, but are more homegrown. I call these low-budget efforts my *"Unfair, Unbalanced, Unedited Series."* But, hey, don't let the series title fool you. We've got some high quality material here that you won't find anywhere else. Listeners tell me I know the right questions to ask my guests, and, hopefully, I get some sensible answers.

Type in *Mr. UFO's Secret Files* on **YouTube.com** and "educate" yourself on the finer points of UFOs and the unexplained cosmos we live in. There are well over 50 "campfire" chats from my *"Route 66"* travels, as well as interviews I have done with outstanding guests on several podcasts I've hosted, plus some interviews

I myself have given on a variety of closely cloistered topics. It's all here under the Big Top and includes a lively discussion with Paul Davids which I call *"A Famous Monster Returns From The Grave,"* in honor of Paul's longtime friendship with the man who actually gave sci-fi its name, Forrest J. Ackerman, both before and after he passed over from the physical world to what we generally term "the afterlife," for lack of better terminology.

Ackerman, as Paul Davids affirms, was a diehard skeptic when it came to anything remotely extrasensory. Now, this isn't hard to believe as most of his friends in the sci-fi and magical communities were nonbelievers to the point of extremism. Isaac Asimov, Ray Bradbury and Arthur C. Clark were "born again" atheists, if there could be such a thing. Joe Moe, Forry's closest friend, summed Ackerman's afterlife "beliefs" up thusly: "Forry was a sworn atheist from his teenaged years on and didn't believe in survival of personality after death. Therefore, he didn't have any romantic illusions about his collection living on beyond him. He simply wanted it to be preserved in his lifetime so he could have the satisfaction of sharing it. Once he was gone, he believed he would never even know that he'd been alive to collect anything."

However, Ackerman did let it be known that, should his thinking processes continue beyond the grave, he would try to communicate with those who were dear to him in life. This is what I call the *"Harry Houdini Pledge,"* which is mostly meaningless when you consider where it comes from. Most magicians and sci-fi buffs believe in little outside of their own imaginary worlds. They take this skepticism as complete gospel, never having spent one single hour as an investigator

Paul Davids, producer, and Tim Beckley

of unexplained phenomena. But they feel no guilt in badmouthing others who have spent their entire lives trying to validate that which ultimately promises a resolution for our souls and the hope of finding peace as we spiritually advance.

But – according to Paul Davids – Forrest J. Ackerman did manage to come back with evidence that there is another world – or worlds – out there that we find ourselves transported to when we clinically die here on earth. First it was a matter of objects seemingly moving about that could not be explained in ordinary terms.

But soon things started to escalate.

How did Davids come to the "irrational" conclusion that his buddy was trying to communicate with him with nonverbal techniques?

Two incidents stand out in Paul's mind, and it's no wonder why!

The first, I guess you could say, was a matter of an "ink blot test."

Davids revealed the details to us and it's up on my YouTube Channel. But I

36

think I will let Tom Ruffles — writing a review of the movie *"The After Life Project,"* which Paul eventually produced — explain the situation, as he did for the prestigious *Society for Psychical Research* in the UK. Ruffles tells the story with admirable, exacting detail.

"On 18 March, 2009, not long after Ackerman's death (he died December 4, 2008), something very odd happened to Davids. While staying alone at his holiday home in Santa Fe, New Mexico, he began printing out a 24-page log of various business meetings and phone calls while he was out. On his return, he picked the sheets up from the printer, placed them on his bed, and left the room. The ink on the sheets was obviously dry. When he returned five minutes later, there was an unusual ink mark, still moist, on the top page, obliterating four words in a single line: 'Spoke to Joe Amodei.' The mark's neatness appeared to indicate intentionality. What is more, it was not uniform. 'Spoke to' could be discerned, but 'Joe Amodei' was completely obscured; Davids had to check the line on his computer. Nothing could have leaked onto the page; he was sure that the document was untouched when he left it on the bed, and such an obvious mark would have been noticeable when he picked it up from the printer. Curiously, for such a significant action, the name Joe Amodei, who is a film producer, meant little to Davids. They had spoken once about a deal that had not taken place but otherwise did not know each other. What could it mean?

"Davids took the page to experts for advice. Jay Siegel, who is the chairman of the chemistry department at the University of Indiana, and John Allison, a chemistry professor at The College of New Jersey, both examined the mysterious mark but could come up with no explanation for how it might have appeared on the paper. After hundreds of hours in the lab, they were unable to recreate its precise appearance. They deduced that the agent blacking out the words was the same as that of the printer ink but contained silver not present in the printer ink. A solvent of some kind had been used to spread the ink and add more than had been on the page to start with, but how, and by whom?"

But this was, as Ruffles reports, only a minor part of the afterlife phenomena.

"The anomalies extended to those involved in the tests. Dr. Allison had been experimenting with various methods trying to recreate the ink mark and had put a batch of pages with his tests on a chair in his dining room, tucked under his briefcase. When he came back into the room to pick up his things, prior to collecting Davids, who was visiting his lab, he found the sheets on the floor, further out than gravity alone would have taken them. This was like Davids' paper episode, with no draught, animal or person around to have done it. Such anecdotes by themselves might not seem particularly convincing to people skeptical of a survival explanation, but it was the first instance of a growing body of incidents that seemed to indicate that Forry was using whatever means were at his disposal to demonstrate that he had survived death."

The **SPR** report states that Davis was so puzzled by this that he arranged for a clairvoyant to come to the house to see what they could pick up. The psychic did find something unusual, Ruffles confirms, as we continue with the anomalies at hand.

"She checked the electro-magnetic fields in the house and found something unusual around a Zimbabwean ceremonial mask that stood in a case just outside the bedroom in which the document was marked. In the film, Davids is shown moving an EMF meter around the case, and the needle is going off the scale. Somewhat unnerved, he moved the mask out of the house, but he mused that Ackerman had a collection of masks and this was an artifact he would have enjoyed. To add to the weirdness, the person who had given him the mask, an inveterate traveler, had a collection of slides of all his journeys, and he discovered that the ones relating to the African trip during which he had acquired the mask had mysteriously disappeared from their neatly stored carousel. No other box had been touched, and the missing slides have never reappeared."

There is another "coincidence," which really blows me away, and which confirms Ackerman's ability to transport himself back to earth to leave clues which confirm an afterlife and which further debunk his atheistic attitude toward the paranormal.

"So far, so strange. But there was more," reasons the **SPR** reviewer. "A week and a half before the ink mark appeared, on 7 March, 2009, a memorial arranged by Joe Moe, who had been Ackerman's personal assistant and caretaker, was held at Hollywood's Egyptian Theater. A documentary made by two Canadian filmmakers, Mike MacDonald and Ian Johnston, *'Famous Monster: Forrest J. Ackerman,'* was shown that evening. Davids spoke at the tribute, and the pair told him afterwards that they had just had some peculiar experiences. While in town, they had a spare day, so they had visited Ackerman's final resting place in Forest Lawn Cemetery and MacDonald, perhaps not in the best of taste, knocked on it, asking if anyone was home, the sort of joke that Forry would have enjoyed. They didn't receive a reply, but returned to the room they were sharing in Hollywood to find their computers doing peculiar things."

Forrest J. Ackerman with GORT.

In order to prove they were real individuals and not robots, they had to type in a random security password on Facebook in order to proceed to their home page. This is where one has to throw "reason" out the window and go along with the concept that synchronicities are not random but more or less part of a "guidance system" operated by interdimensional intelligence, which would most likely include members of those Heavenly realms we are so interested in connecting with UFO visitors. And, remember, Forry Ackerman had alien figures from such sci-fi classics as *"The Day The Earth Stood Still"* and models of spaceships from many a movie all on display behind glass cases in the various rooms of his **"Famous Monsters"** Hollywood estate, which travelers from all over the world visited.

The **SPR** review continues thus:

"The code that they had to retype? 'Ackerman 000,' and the first letter was initialized. As they were absorbing this and saying some of the things that might have come up onscreen, one of them said 'Ackerman dead,' whereupon Johnston's computer, supposedly in sleep mode, suddenly yelled 'Oh, my God, no way!' This was the voice of an animated character on YouTube, but he did not have YouTube open on his computer at the time. It seemed to be a comment, echoing their thoughts, on what had just happened with Facebook. What made it even odder was that Johnston had a photograph of Ackerman, aged about four and a half, on his computer which he had uploaded when working on the documentary, an age appropriate to the childish voice which said 'Oh, my God, no way!' The computer events were within 30 seconds of each other, less than an hour after MacDonald knocked on Ackerman's tomb."

Paul Davids apparently was told about this on March 8th, ten days before the ink blot appeared, and it was really at this point that Davids started to see a pattern emerge, one that pointed directly to the discarnate Forest J. Ackerman. The significance of the blacked-out line was still not apparent.

"It was only when speaking to Joe Moe to find out about Ackerman's editing practices that he realized that 'Joe Moe' was contained in 'Joe Amodei.' Ackerman had loved puns, using them extensively in his writing, and this was precisely the sort of wordplay that he would have enjoyed. Was this the reason why that line alone had been affected, Ackerman literally 'dropping him a line?' As if in confirmation, Moe then told Davids that a few days after the memorial, he had had a vivid dream in which Ackerman had appeared to him and praised the gathering, calling it the '9th wonder of the World' (King Kong, of course, being the 8th). So it would seem that Ackerman contacted Joe in his dream and then Davids, to tell him, 'Spoke to Joe Moe.' Davids later found that, when editing, Ackerman often deleted sentences in exactly the same way as on his paper."

By no means does Paul Davids think that the issue at hand is "random" or a mere "coincidence." The Hollywood Renaissance man believes, as he puts it in an interview for Australia's **New Dawn** magazine, that he was "targeted" by Forry Ackerman.

"I think the incident of the inkblot is VERY important. Sometimes the answers to very big cosmic mysteries come in very small packages. Scientists deal at the level of individual atoms and sub-atomic particles. Others study photons or very faint astronomical phenomena from far off in space that have been traveling toward earth for billions of years. My first question was, does the blacking out of four words in my document, at two separate levels of opacity, contain clues as to its origin that can tell us how it was done or why it was done? Is there something 'paranormal' about it that can be demonstrated?

"The four words on my document were clearly targeted and the ink obliteration was deliberate and done by 'someone' or 'something' other than me while I was out of the room, at a time when NO ONE else was physically present in the house. I knew this for a fact, but could I convince anyone else? It actually surprises me the overwhelming extent to which the two key chemists who worked on it (one of them, Dr. John Allison, continued the work for years) state categorically that it is still a huge mystery they cannot explain and cannot duplicate in any way they can conceive – and they have tried hundreds of ways to duplicate it. Both Dr. Allison and Dr. Jay Siegel are world class authorities on the chemistry of inks, paints and solvents. Dr. Siegel has testified in a massive number of court cases where someone was needed to testify about the chemistry of evidence."

And so there you pretty much have it, the whole ball of afterlife wax in a fascinating happening that occurred to someone I know and trust. And all this so impressed Paul Davids that he went out and produced *"The After Life Project,"* a two volume DVD set that originally aired on the **SyFy** cable channel and is now available to home consumers.

There are many other "strange incidents" that have found their way into this book, but before it's possible to conceive that UFOs can act as a conduit between this life and the next, we need to verify that the likelihood that we continue on to another space and time is within the realm of "reason," even if science refuses to look at the empirical evidence that Diane Tessman, Sean Casteel and I have collected from those who have spent years in the verification process.

FURTHER INFORMATION AND VALIDATION AVAILABLE AT . . .

www.TheLifeAfterDeathProject.com

www.spr.ac.uk/publication/life-after-death-project-dvd

www.PaulDavids.com

Teenage "Monster Movie Maker" Paul Davids (left) and his "co-producer" Jeff Tinsley create creatures for one of their childhood 8mm films. They won Honorable Mention in Forry Ackerman's first Famous Monsters Amateur Movie contest, and that sent Paul on his way to an eventual Hollywood career.

Paul Davids and his mentor the late Forry Ackerman — has he contacted Paul from the other side?

The After Life Project DVD lays out all the evidence that the "Famous Monsters" editor is not just idle in his new home.

"Every soul has existed from the beginning; it has therefore passed through some worlds already, and will pass through others before it reaches the final consummation. It comes into the world strengthened by the victories or weakened by the defeats of its previous life."

—ORIGEN (Early Christian Scholar)

LIFE AFTER DEATH: WE SET SAIL INTO THE COSMOS!
BY DIANE TESSMAN

Update: It's been over thirty years since I first researched the possibility of life after death. Today, I find this Question of the Ages to be even more intriguing; the implications and possibilities are mind boggling!

Are some UFO occupants actually human souls who have traveled forward to a new level of existence? Or are UFOs themselves actually human spirits blazing across the skies as they celebrate their new, higher level of life?

Of course there are many diverse and equally mind-bending sources and origins of UFOs and their occupants, whether it is extraterrestrials from far distant planets, a form of plasma life or human time travelers. After all these years, we still do not know the truth about UFOs. However, I now consider the very real possibility that the UFO phenomenon is an aspect of our own immortality, our own life after death.

Many UFOs morph in ever-changing forms; they seem to be composed of a vibrating plasma or liquid-like energy. This sounds very much like an angelic form of life! The knowledge that angels exist is as old as the human race. Might UFO beings, having shed the shackles of physical human life, manifest as this angel-energy so that we might perceive them?

The question is simple: Is the brain all we've got? Or do we have a mind and spirit which are not dependent on our physical body but which simply nestle in the physical folds of the brain all the years?

It is likely that our soul is not a ball of light somewhere in our torso, but rather our soul is the living spirit within every DNA particle of our body. We do not have a small ball of light within us, we ARE a blazing light! This is our essence. Who is to say what form or shape our blazing essence will take after it leaves our body?

Our brain seems to be similar to the pipes of a plumbing network, but our consciousness is the water which runs through these pipes. When the pipes "die," the water races outward; it does not die too. Our unique spirit sails into the infinite cosmic field of quantum consciousness.

Throughout the universe there are plasma networks like magnificent spider webs; in fact, all galaxies are connected with electric threads of plasma. Electromagnetic energy is also the energy within our brains. We might compare our brains to a television set; the power to run them comes from the field of electromagnetic universal quantum consciousness.

The universe is a magnificent living consciousness! We are all sparks of this living consciousness.

Where does reincarnation fit in? Perhaps the individual's immortal essence chooses to live another lifetime as a human or even as one of Earth's animals, while others choose to travel to the "UFO dimension" or to the angelic realms. One thing is sure: consciousness goes on and on!

My question to mainstream science: Do you assume that, when the brain dies with the rest of the physical body, the individual's consciousness dies too? Or that that consciousness never existed? Considering the incredible research in quantum physics into consciousness itself, can you actually state that the brain is all we've got?

Those who have had near-death-experiences report finding their consciousness expanding outside the boundaries of their bodies. They say that the feeling is like taking off a tight shoe or an uncomfortable suit of armor. They report that this experience is more real than waking reality. They report feeling that the vastness and beauty of their new perception is beyond words, beyond the ability of any human language to fully explain. Thousands of documented cases prove that near-death-experiencers can report accurately on what happened to their bodies when they were clinically dead, with no brain waves and in cardiac arrest. Their consciousness began to travel on!

Look out of your eyes; your consciousness is perceiving this reality. Your consciousness has the ability to perceive other realities. Your brain is the filter which dictates that you perceive this reality, but, when your physical brain dies, your consciousness is free to perceive all which is out there. You can settle into a new physical body or you can remain a universal traveler.

It is thrilling to realize that we humans are reaching the step in our evolution wherein Science and Spirituality meet and become one. There should be no contradiction, no on-going argument between those who think scientifically and those who feel and think spiritually. A rainbow is a prism of light caused by the sun shining on raindrops to the scientist, but to one who is spiritual, the rainbow is a symbol of hope.

Why do we humans always have to bicker about who is right? In fact, the rainbow is both. Science and Spirit harmonize with each other to create a reality which is larger than the sum of its two parts. As we evolve, we realize this truth and find joy in the wonder of the universe!

I firmly believe that one of the greatest wonders of the universe is the truth that our living consciousness is immortal. We are infinite. I am sure that at some point on our timeless cosmic path, our spirit travels in a morphing, shining vessel through Earth skies.

info@earthchangepredictions.com

Enjoy my new book, "THE UFO AGENDA, SO...YOU WANT TO KNOW THE TRUTH?"

http://www.amazon.com/The-UFO-Agenda-ebook/dp/B00DUEPPJ4

Or, you can order UFO AGENDA in paperback form directly from me and I will personally autograph it for you. Write to me at Diane Tessman, P.O. Box 352, St. Ansgar, Iowa, 50472

I will send you free samples of my 2 publications THE STAR NETWORK HEARTLINE and THE CHANGE TIMES QUARTERLY (current issues!). Write to my postal address or contact me online! Specify if you wish paper or online copies.

I offer Transition Counseling. With my higher contact Tibus, I help people deal with the fact that we all "die," and that we all are getting older ("closer to death") every day. Sometimes my clients have a terminal disease; other times they are healthy people who simply want guidance in the mystical and spiritual phenomenon of "death." I firmly believe "death" is simply the bridge to new life, one step up the awareness ladder. Tell me of your concerns and problems. I also counsel star seeds and contactees; I have over 32 years of counseling experience. My readings and/or counseling via mail or email are $100, comprehensive, private, and personal. Let me help you. dianetessman0@gmail.com

Diane Tessman at Joshua Tree

OUR CATS AND DOGS DO REINCARNATE BACK TO US!
BY DIANE TESSMAN

Our beloved dog loves us unconditionally! Our beautiful cat seems independent and nonchalant, but, when you lay down at night, she shows her timeless love and devotion for you, her human.

So many of my friends have said to me, "When my dog passed on, it hit me like a death in the family. It indeed was a death in the family because this dog of mine was so exceptional and wonderful! She was an integral part of this family!"

Our animal friends go to heaven and what's more, they reincarnate back to us sometimes!

Many years ago, we didn't dare say publically that when they die, our dogs and cats go over the rainbow bridge to a perfect green home wherein they can romp and run as they did when they were puppies and kittens; in other words, they go to heaven just as we do. We were taught by religions that only humans go to heaven and we were not to love a mere animal so much.

Fortunately, these days, we are free to express our belief that animals too go to heaven because society has acknowledged how important and special our pets are to us. Also, we realize that animals have intelligence far beyond what they were thought to possess years ago. In fact, we don't even like to use the word "pet" anymore because we truly feel they are simply members of our family.

In my many years of exploring life after death and other spiritual mysteries, I have discovered that there is much more to "life after death" for our animal friends. I believe some animal friends do begin a new life in a heavenly spiritual place, but others choose to return to Earth as a new lifeform; twice in a while, a beloved pet chooses to return to their human (you!) as a new friend and companion.

Of all my experiences with the paranormal, of all my UFO sightings and even my childhood extraterrestrial encounters, the greatest, most emotionally moving proof of my own immortality has been given to me by my dog Hannah and my cat Pavarotti. I will tell you their stories in a moment.

Hannah and The Pooka have taught me that old physics lesson: energy is changed but never destroyed. Therefore, the energy of life itself never dies, it only changes form! Speaking of an "afterlife" is not accurate because life simply goes on; life is life! Life itself continues in heaven, or in a new lifetime. For some pets, life begins anew in a new fur suit. Reincarnation!

I hasten to add that some humans and some animals wish to graduate to a non-physical form of life; these are often wise old souls who have had many lifetimes on Earth and who are now ready for The Cosmos and its energy kingdom. They are tired of the hassles of Earth and have reached a level of enlightenment which allows their consciousness, still in its unique, individual form, to sail away.

However, our dogs and cats can and do come back to us in reincarnated form! They often do not want go to a new life in The Cosmos without their beloved human. Also, they may still need to experience physical life on Earth. Of course this is also true of humans: some of us wish to travel on past daily life on Earth, while others of us choose to incarnate in new life on Earth.

How is this decision made? I feel this depends on cosmic forces we cannot fully comprehend except when it is time to do so. Our dogs, cats, and other animal friends possess a simple unconditional love, and so I feel their choice may be easier than our complex human choice. Of course the level of enlightenment of the lifeform determines this also.

Diane and her Irish Labrador, Sinsee

SINSEE BECOMES HANNAH, MY REINCARNATED ANGEL-DOG

In Ireland in 1990, my daughter and I got an adorable yellow Labrador puppy who my daughter named Sinsee. Sinsee was not a rescue dog, as were most of my animals. She was from championship British and American stock. The woman who bred this amazing Labrador family explained to us that this particular puppy was born dead and that she had performed mouth to mouth resuscitation on the dead puppy for three minutes until the newborn angel sprang to life.

Sinsee lived for fifteen glorious years. We often said that she was actually in charge of our family; she was super-intelligent, super-funny, super-helpful. She was indeed an angel dog!

Sinsee came back with us from Ireland in 1995, along with fifteen cats and our St. Bernard. We landed at JFK Airport, New York City, and then drove a U-Haul truck across country to our new home in Joshua Tree, California. Our many animal friends were right with us.

When we moved back to my native North Iowa in 1997, our Sinsee rode "shotgun" in the pick-up truck. It was in Iowa that I started our Iowa Star Network Animal Sanctuary which is still thriving today. (Donations welcomed!)

Sinsee passed on in October, 2004. However, just before she passed, I received a telepathic message from her. She whispered, "I will come back to you, but this time I will be a hardship case." "Hardship case" is not an expression I use often and I am positive this did not come from my own mind! It refers to the fact that Sinsee came from championship stock; she had never known a bad day, never been hurt, never gone hungry or homeless as so many dogs do.

In December 2004, my daughter and I went to the Humane Society of North Iowa to look for a new puppy. My daughter fell in love with "Freddi," and we adopted her; I became mesmerized by another puppy. I was not allowed to go up to her but had to stay in another room because this puppy had a horrendous staph infection. She had been used as bait in a dog fighting ring, said the Humane Society; she was only about 8 weeks old. They also told me that the people who brought

her in had not bothered to do so for many days and so the staph infection had become really terrible.

Photo shows the scars Hannah still has, staph run-off scars on legs, and actual teeth marks

This beautiful little puppy's right side and face were deeply torn up and looked like raw hamburger. In all her pain, the puppy

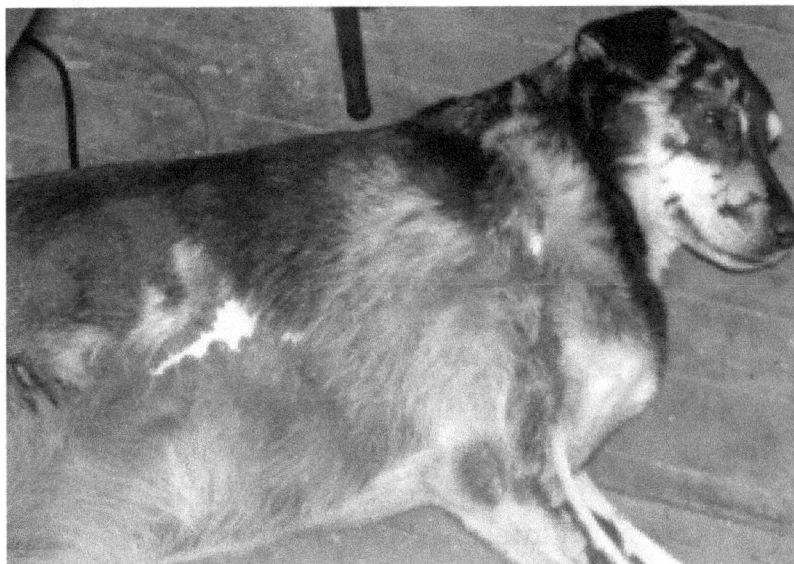

49

gazed at me and I gazed back. I said quietly to her, "Sinsee? What a hardship case you are!"

The Humane Society had named her "Hannah" and so I telepathically promised Hannah that if she lived, I would adopt her. Hannah fought to live for 3 months. The Humane Society insisted on keeping her for the duration. Her wonderful foster mother took care of her daily. Much of the time Hannah could not even move but wagged her tail. The vet considered amputating her right front leg by her gnawed shoulder but did not; it does have a permanent staple in it.

Finally, Hannah was miraculously healed and ready to be adopted. Her foster mother wanted to keep Hannah but Hannah kept telling her, "Thanks for all you have done, but I don't belong to you." Her foster mother sensed that Hannah belonged to me and so phoned me to ask if I was ready to adopt her. Was I ever ready!

Sinsee had indeed reincarnated as Hannah! I firmly believe that Hannah would not have lived if the strong, loving spirit of Angel Sinsee had not gone into her, fortifying and healing her!

As my reincarnated "new" dog ran into my home for the first time, she already knew the layout of my house. She acted as if she had lived here for many years – and indeed she had (as Sinsee). The other dogs and cats greeted her as an old friend.

Hannah and her favorite cats

I know a skeptic would say that I am simply telling myself this story but there is a lot of proof that Sinsee did reincarnate as Hannah. Let me give you one small example out of many bits of proof:

Several years after I got Hannah, I was talking to a friend about my five years in Ireland. When I lived in rural Kilkenny, a pre-teen neighbor named Mary Francis cared for Sinsee and my other animals when I was gone for a few days. I mentioned the name "Mary Francis" to my friend in calm, normal conversation and I did not even think of the fact Hannah was sitting there. Immediately Hannah bounded up, jumping up and down for joy because Sinsee always responded to Mary Francis' name; she loved to hear that Mary Francis was coming to our house.

Hannah of course was never in Ireland, she never knew Mary Francis.

Hannah today: Her good looking left side

* * * * *

Now, here is the story of my reincarnated cat!

SAKIMA REINCARNATES TO THE POOKA CAT:

Like cats, this tale is very detailed and complex, and so I will simply tell you that Sakima came to me in 1984 when I lived in Poway, California, under strange but wonderful circumstances. I took him to Ireland in 1989 along with other animal friends.

Sakima passed on in Ireland in 1993; he had been very special to me. A short while later, my neighbor Mary Francis found a tiny kitten in bad shape who had beautiful silver and black marmalade fur, just like Sakima. Her parents did not have money to buy antibiotics but I couldn't just steal this kitten, whom I desperately wanted to save, from the neighbor girl.

One day I stopped by my neighbor's small general store for a second, then drove on home about three miles in my old car. About an hour later, I looked out the window, and there was this tiny sick kitten climbing out from the underneath framework of my car!

I nursed him to health with antibiotics, keeping him warm in a small plastic tub. It soon became clear that he had all the small unique behaviors of Sakima. Only a fellow cat lover would know how one cat has entirely different habits and quirks than other cats. This kitten was absolutely identical to Sakima! I named him The Pooka after a magic Celt legend. He reincarnated because he and I had bonded in a special cosmic way which is difficult to put into mere words.

If you have not considered that a new animal friend might be the reincarnation of a much-loved animal friend who has passed on, stop to consider this. Of course a new friend can be himself and be wonderful on his own. If there is a possibility that your new friend is the reincarnation of your old friend, remember that he need not be the same breed of dog, need not be the same color of cat. However, you, as your animal's beloved human, might notice first one small hint and then another which tells you this is the same soul!

Dogs and cats are high on the spiritual ladder – they simply love, unconditionally! Animals know more than we do about the mysterious workings of nature

51

and consciousness. Animals do reincarnate, they do have souls and they do go to heaven. I pray the day will come when all dogs and cats have loving homes because they truly bless our lives.

Diane and The Pooka

We deeply appreciate your donation to our Star Network Animal Sanctuary on ten lovely green acres in North Iowa. Winters get down to 40 degrees below zero here and there is NO animal shelter in this county! We give many cats their forever home right here. Write for information. dianetessman0@gmail.com Diane Tessman, P.O. Box 352, St. Ansgar, IA, 50472

WHAT DO HEAVEN AND UFOS
REALLY HAVE TO DO WITH EACH OTHER?

Who, if anybody, should be blamed for the tragic situation in which 39 people took their own lives because they believed that they were simply shedding their earthly bodies ("containers," they called them) in order to return to their starship, which they believed was traveling behind the Hale-Bopp Comet?

Before giving our answers to these important questions, it should be noted that the mass media jumped on this unfortunate event like hungry barracudas, digging into the fact that some male members of the Heaven's Gate group were surgically castrated.

Immediately, the press put a negative slant on anything to do with this "cult," including the fact that its leader had once been involved in a gay relationship when he was a college music professor and that he had met his "soul-mate" in a mental institution.

Regardless of how one personally feels about gay relationships, it is certain that the media hit new heights in hypocrisy when, in one breath, they give "politically correct" lip service to the right of consenting adults to love whom they please, and, with the next breath, smirk about the fact the group's leader, named Do (formerly known as Bo) had a homosexual relationship years previously and felt guilty about it. And while men of all faiths and denominations have had to tangle with such "demons," isn't it, in reality, the so-called orthodox religions, and not the supposed cult groups, that make us feel guilty and insecure when it comes to our own individual sexuality? So much so that it is not that uncommon for the religiously inclined to take matters into their own hands and torture themselves either spiritually or physically due to their own individual leanings.

What the same media, as well as those who consider themselves to be "cult hunters," neglect to mention is that the people who originally drove the group's leader into a mental institution did so because they didn't understand his fascination with UFOs and extraterrestrials.

Sometimes, society can "condemn" us without reasonable cause, simply because they do not possess the knowledge to deal with what they see as differences of opinion and individual thinking that may go against what is at that time considered to be the "norm."

Can we also, in all honesty, hold our own government to blame? It would seem that they may be in reality a cause of the hysteria that has grown up around the whole idea of UFOs simply because, for the last half a century, they have decided it is their duty to hide the truth from the public for its own "protection."

Because of this, society has had to formulate its own preconceptions and conclusions about something which they inwardly know to be real due to personal observation and experience.

Many of us have a tough time dealing with something which society's great institutions tell us we should shun . . . the same institutions we have been led to believe are always infallible.

On the videos which were left behind, Do's followers – known as "monks" – appear to be very intelligent and enlightened, to have a great sense of humor and camaraderie. Yet we are told that they are kooks and crackpots. The fundamental question must be: why does society condemn such people outright, even making them the brunt of sad jokes, while at the same time traditional Christian beliefs are based around a man who was ostracized in his time, a man who had fiercely devoted followers, who was more intelligent, enlightened and gentle than the world around him?

Traditional Christianity teaches us that if you are good, you will go to heaven, which is a place of perfection where none of the worldly woes exist. Heaven is "up there" somewhere, amongst the stars, comets and planets. Catholic monks and nuns are considered by some to be very worthy spiritual people. But apparently, there is a "copyright" on who can be a monk. If you are not of a huge, multi-billion-dollar church conglomerate, your right to consider yourself a "monk" is not valid because then you are just a cult member.

This is what we are repeatedly being told, but is this necessarily true? What separates the big churches from the cults? Is it the number of followers and the amount of their bank balance which determines our feelings toward them? A century or so ago the Mormons were considered to be a cult (remember how their leader Joseph Smith was persecuted?), while today they are thought of in much more "traditional" terms.

HEAVEN ABOUNDS FOR THE FAITHFUL

When someone passes on, traditional belief tells us to rejoice, that he or she has gone on to a higher place. But when Heaven's Gate members die, video cameras cruelly, intrusively scan their lifeless physical forms, and narrators sorrowfully tell us how pitiful their deaths are. We are told that they are dead as dead can be, that their plans to go to a higher place were nothing but a big deception.

What if someone were to say such negative things about a person at a traditional funeral? Every aspect of Heaven's Gate's beliefs have been ridiculed and dissected. Isn't it time society learned to be more tolerant of a person's right to independence, though that independence might take them away from the norm? After all, isn't individuality what America is supposed to be all about?

Perhaps this double standard is the very thing Heaven's Gate members found wrong with society. Perhaps this is why they chose to live together in a monastery away from the world that had rejected them and their beliefs out of hand.

We do not feel that society should condone or condemn others without having spent a day in their shoes. Traditionally, we have been taught that suicide is wrong, but should we not be sympathetic with the hurt and anger which anyone who considers suicide must feel?

It seems like Heaven's Gate members should have stayed on Earth to assist in this planet's transformation period, which is likely to be the greatest crisis civilization has ever gone through. It would seem that they "deserted" right when we needed their enlightenment, intelligence and gentleness the most. Despite all our doubtful thoughts, we must still ask the question: Can a UFO take us to heaven?

This little book attempts to answer this and other relevant questions that are all-too-important as we enter these days shortly after the change of the millennium. Many do not comprehend that there are indeed various levels of consciousness. Quantum physics tells us about multi-dimensions and there is now even "scientific" proof that different and various realms abound throughout the cosmos. Every individual must learn to cherish his or her freedom of choice.

To truly accomplish a higher consciousness, free will must be present. There can be no cult leader who says he or she is your savior. You must learn that your savior is within yourself! Look to spiritual teachers and friends, if you must, for guidance and input, but do not let them dictate to you. Do NOT let them demand to be worshiped. You are your own country and, as such, you have the right to issue your own Passport to Heaven!

Such actions as mass suicide, in our view, do not lend themselves to evolving to a higher consciousness. To place your sacred life force in a leader's hands is not an act of wisdom or higher awareness but a cop-out.

In this book, the authors give insight on what are undoubtedly the most fascinating, urgent questions of today: Is there life after death? Are there other realms of existence? And how can a person get to the uppermost places?

In this time of planetary crisis, these questions haunt us more and more. Millions of people have seen and encountered UFOs, so we are not in a position to laugh at them anymore. Do these craft return to the higher levels of existence once they leave Earth? Have the occupants of UFOs – whom some identify as aliens, and others recognize as angels – graduated to a realm which is more heavenly and beyond our daily existence? And is it possible we can join them?

The deaths in San Diego make us ask these questions with even more curiosity and an increased sense of urgency. What must each and every one of us know, feel and believe as the early years of the new millennium draw to a close? Allow us to tell you about Your Passport to Heaven!

Diane Tessmann

We ask that you read this book with an open mind and appreciate all comments meant in good faith while rejecting all that come from negativity. The angelic kingdom awaits us all and our personal guardian angels are here to offer protection and guidance. No one can benefit from close-minded ignorance.

Timothy Green Beckley

Each person is at each moment capable of re-membering all that has ever happened to him and of perceiving everything that is happening every-where in the universe. The function of the brain and nervous systems is to protect us from being over-whelmed and confused by this mass of largely use-less and irrelevant knowledge, by shutting out most of what we should otherwise perceive or remem-ber at any moment, and leaving only that very small and special selection which is likely to be practical and useful.

The "real" world "outside" is not at all what our senses tell us it is. It consists mainly of swirls and buzzes and booms of pure energy. The laws of phys-ics tell us that the building blocks of all that we see as solid are, in fact, insubstantial points of energy.

Reality is a hologram generated internally by the brain. It is, in every sense, Maya—the Advaita Vedanta belief that "reality" does not exist outside the human mind, and is grounded in the quantum physics interpretation whereby "reality" is brought into existence by the act of observation.

Charon leaned forward and rowed. All things were one with his weariness.

It was not with him a matter of years or of centuries, but of wide floods of time, and an old heaviness and a pain in the arms that had become for him part of the scheme that the gods had made and was of a piece with Eternity.

If the gods had even sent him a contrary wind it would have divided all time in his memory into two equal slabs.

So grey were all things always where he was that if any radiance lingered a moment among the dead, on the face of such a queen perhaps as Cleopatra, his eyes could not have perceived it.

It was strange that the dead nowadays were coming in such numbers. They were coming in thousands where they used to come in fifties. It was neither Charon's duty nor his wont to ponder in his grey soul why these things might be. Charon leaned forward and rowed.

Then no one came for a while. It was not unusual for the gods to send no one down from Earth for such a space. But the gods knew best.

Then one man came alone. And the little shade sat shivering on a lonely bench and the great boat pushed off. Only one passenger; the gods knew best.

And great and weary Charon rowed on and on beside the little, silent, shivering ghost.

And the sound of the river was like a mighty sigh that Grief in the beginning had sighed among her sisters, and that could not die like the echoes of human sorrow failing on earthly hills, but was as old as time and the pain in Charon's arms.

Then the boat from the slow, grey river loomed up to the coast of Dis and the little, silent shade still shivering stepped ashore, and Charon turned the boat to go wearily back to the world. Then the little shadow spoke, that had been a man.

"I am the last," he said.

No one had ever made Charon smile before, no one before had ever made him weep.

"Have you ever had a dream, Neo, that you were so sure was real? What if you were unable to wake from that dream? How would you know the difference between the dream world and the real world?"

—MORPHEUS (The Matrix)

LIFE – NOT DEATH – AFTER LIFE!

There is no doubt the heavens await . . . Bright angels have from glory come; They're round my bed, they're in my room, They wait to waft my spirit home! All is well! All is well!

In the course of the author's spiritual counseling work, we have had many letters from people wondering if there is indeed life after death. Very often these people have just lost a loved one and they seek hope and encouragement on the phenomenon of "death" and the afterlife. We have both also been in touch with other people telling of their own life-after-death experiences. In some cases, they tell of their own near death, of the glorious other world they saw and of their reluctant return to life in this dimension.

In other instances, they tell of their personal experiences following the death of a loved one, of how the loved one reappeared from the other dimension in order to let the person left behind know that there is indeed life – not death – after life!

SCIENCE AND RELIGION IN HARMONY

It is the hope of Tim Beckley and Diane Tessman that this book will give the reader reassurance that the spirit does not cease to exist. Both science and religion now appear to agree on this point. Consider the fact that Albert Einstein revealed that energy cannot be destroyed, it can only be changed into other forms. Also consider the fact that all spiritual beliefs in the world, be they eastern or western, Christian or non-Christian, teach us that life is a sacred and indestructible energy. All religions tell us, in various terms, that the special essence unique to each individual called "the soul" does live on.

Some beliefs tell us that the soul goes to the dimension of heaven, while other beliefs tell us that the soul is reborn into another physical being, to continue its journey through the cosmos. The details of where the soul goes and what it does after death vary, but the basic tenet that the soul does not die is universal.

61

And so, science and religion both reassure us, despite their different terminology, that there is life after death – but can we have a real and true picture of exactly what does happen? Let's see what science and religion have to say.

A SCIENTIST OFFERS PROOF OF SURVIVAL

At some time in their life, everyone is asked the question: Do you believe you will go on living after you die? Well, do you believe it? Consider the facts. Time after time people have reported that a dying person's face is suddenly filled with HAPPINESS at the actual moment of death. Is it possible to know WHY? Yes. Through the people who have experienced "death" – and come back to tell the story. This enquiry begins with the documented evidence of a scientist. He has made the most careful study yet of WHAT HAPPENS WHEN PEOPLE DIE.

He is Dr. Robert Crookall, who lives in Dursley, Gloucestershire. He has probed and sifted through all the cases he could track down. Here are some of them:

CASE of the man who lost a bond acknowledging a debt of money. Without the bond he could not legally demand repayment. His debtor repudiated the claim. Then he was almost drowned. Scene by scene, his life passed before him – INCLUDING THE MOMENT WHEN HE HAD HIDDEN THE BOND IN A SECRET PLACE. When he recovered he went to his bookcase, took out a book and extracted the bond.

CASE of Flight-Lieut. J.P. Wynton. He described to Dr. Crookall how he experienced a timeless review of his life as he crashed in a plane and was almost burnt to death. But, from the pilot and others, Dr. Cookall made a new and strange discovery. Time after time, people snatched from violent death told him that as death approached they felt no pain.

His theory was confirmed by another similar instance. CASE of Leslie Grant Scott. "Dying is not such a terrifying thing," said Mr. Scott. "I died and came back. I found death one of the easiest things in life."

Or, again, consider: CASE of a man who fell from a tremendous height. He said: "When my body finally bounded against the rocks, I became unconscious without experiencing any pain whatever. The moments when I stood at the brink of the (new) life were the happiest I ever experienced."

Dr. Crookall also listened to the CASE of a doctor who fell a hundred feet, heard the noise when his head struck various corners of rocks, but stated: "In all this I felt no pain." This only came later when he reentered his body.

These cases and many others were published in a book written by Dr. Crookall called "The Supreme Adventure." Dr. Crookall is a scientist. He has been demonstrator in botany at Aberdeen University and Principal Geologist to Her Majesty's Geological Survey. He likes to go about things in a scientific way. He decided that we were looking for proof of survival in the wrong place. If we wanted evidence about the next world we should look for it there, not in verifiable memories of this world.

He began by collecting communications from the "dead" by whatever means they came. He examined thousands of accounts of what these allegedly dead people said they experienced at, and soon after, death. From these he was able to build up the first consistent and coherent account of how those who have been through death say they pass from this world to the next. This is the amazing picture which emerged:

1. In addition to his Physical Body, man also has a Psychical or Soul Body which we cannot see or touch but which has the same shape as the physical body. And there is another Spiritual Body, too, on a higher level still.

2. As a man approaches a natural death, at old age, his thoughts fly instinctively to friends who have died already. He summons them to help him over to the next stage.

3. Near the moment of death, man experiences a detailed review of his past earthly life.

4. About an hour before visible death, when the heart stops beating and he ceases to breathe, a dying man has often already left his physical body and stands nearby conscious and happy. This is what we call the pre-death coma.

5. Natural death involves no physical pain or fear.

6. Many of the newly dead do not, for a time, realize that they have shed their physical bodies.

7. The psychical double that leaves the physical body at death usually floats for a while horizontally around the dead physical body, resembles it, and looks younger and brighter,.

8. Many of the newly dead see immediately friends who have died already, especially those whom they have unconsciously called.

9. When he has severed the final links with his physical body, the average man who dies naturally has a recuperative sleep lasting for three or four days of our time. But a man who is killed in the prime of life tends to be awake at once.

10. The next world in which he finds himself is not, as is taught in some churches, of a purely spiritual nature, or the Paradise of the Bible. That comes later. The next world for the average man is semi-physical in nature: intermediate

between our earth and the "Heaven" of the Scriptures. It is earth-like and familiar.

11. During the period which follows, the newly dead man experiences a second review of his past earth life. This time emotional, selective and responsible. It is the Biblical "Judgement."

12. On the basis of this each person goes eventually to his own place in the spiritual or super-physical heavens. These cannot be described in normal language, but they are more real than the physical world.

SUDDEN OR VIOLENT DEATH

But what happens to the people who die a sudden or violent death? They suffer from shock, says Dr. Crookall. For them it is difficult to realize what happened. But with help, after a period of rest in special conditions after death, they are ready to join the normal sequence. The first question Dr. Crookall asked, as a scientist, was: "DOES IT MAKE SENSE?" He found that it does.

More than that, he found the communications he tested were consistent with one another. Then he discovered something even more conclusive. It was possible to test the sensations said to be experienced by newly dead people by comparing them with sensations known to have been experienced by people who have returned from near death to physical life.

The communications from the dead said that they actually left their bodies about an hour before the heart stopped beating. And that while they were still linked by the invisible cord to their physical bodies, it was always possible to return to them. During this period, people who did return, and are alive today, have experienced some of the first stages of the transition from this life to the next. That's where these cases we showed you at the start come in. For these experiences are similar, usually identical, to those described by the dead.

Many people who have "died" and come back have described how they left their physical body and looked down on it. And this has been corroborated by people who have never been near death themselves but have seen it happen while watching others die.

Let us examine another case. CASE of an American doctor, R.B. Hout, of Indiana. At the deathbed of his aunt he saw "this astral body hang suspended horizontally a few feet above the physical counterpart. It was quiet, serene and in repose. But the physical body was active in reflex movements and subconscious writhing in pain. I saw the features plainly. They were very similar to the physical face except that a glow of peace and vigor was expressed instead of age and pain. My uncle, the deceased husband of my aunt, stood there beside her bed. Also her son, passed away many years previously."

This phase – the arrival of friends or relatives already dead – has been corroborated by almost everyone who has seen death often. Time after time, the dying person's face is suddenly filled with happiness at the actual moment of death. Sometimes they even speak the name of a friend or relation who has died before.

Crookall found that "there seems to be no single case on record in which a dying person claimed to see a living friend whom he erroneously thought to be dead. On the other hand, there are many recorded cases of dying people who saw friends whom they supposed to be living and who were in fact dead."

Doctors are so used to this phenomenon that some have come to expect death soon after their patients appear to see friends who have died.

A NURSE'S EXPERIENCE

A nurse with twenty years' experience has testified: "I notice that often just before the end, the dying would seem to recognize someone who was not of those at the bedside and who was unseen by the latter. I have seen a woman who had been in a coma for hours suddenly open her eyes with a look of glad surprise, stretch forth her hands as though to grasp invisible hands outstretched towards her, and then, with a sigh of relief, expire.

"That at such moments the dying really see some spirit form – someone who has come from the other world to welcome them – I have never doubted."

Perhaps you are one of those who are in doubt. Everyone who believes in Christianity should, as an act of faith, believe that they will survive their own death. Yet, recent surveys have revealed that more than half the people of Britain have no conviction at all. Faith and the evidence of the Bible are no longer enough. They want proof. Others like the nurse and Dr. Hout, of Indiana, who have come face to face with the evidence, have no more doubts. And Dr. Crookall, in the face of the body of evidence he has amassed, was unable to doubt either.

"The whole of the available evidence," he concludes, "is explicable only on the hypothesis of the survival of the human soul in a Soul Body. There is no longer a deadlock or stalemate on the question of survival. On the contrary, survival is as well-established as the theory of evolution."

OTHER SCIENTISTS REPORT THEIR OBSERVATIONS

The majority of the readers of this book are probably very familiar with the fine research done by Raymond A. Moody, Jr., M.D., whose book "Life After Life" topped the bestseller list several years ago. Yet these same readers may not be familiar with the excellent investigative techniques applied by other men of science, who, though they might have started out as skeptics, are now convinced of survival.

Take as an example the investigation conducted by Dr. Kenneth Ring, a professor of psychology at the University of Connecticut. As co-founder and First Vice-President of the Association for the Scientific Study of Near-Death Phenomena, Dr. Ring has interviewed more than a hundred men and women who have come very close to death or have experienced what is termed "clinical death," a state in which vital signs such as heartbeat and respiration have been entirely absent from their bodies.

In his book *"Life at Death"* (Coward, McCann & Geoghegan), Dr. Ring confirms the findings made by researchers before him in this area, including the following sensations which have commonly been associated with those undergoing a near death experience:

A sense of floating out of one's body. The feeling of flying through a dark tunnel at whose end there is a brilliant white light. Experiencing a review of one's life, the scenes flashing before the mind's eye in rapid order.

Not quick to draw conclusions of his own, Dr. Ring does seem adequately impressed by the weight of experience he has seen and in his first literary effort he shows that the near-death-experience is not affected by an individual's age, education, race or religion. He found instead that the typical near-death-experience – which he terms a "core experience" – tends to unfold in a series of five stages. The "deeper" the stage, the fewer the people who reach it.

The experience tends, Dr. Ring maintains, to end with an encounter with what is often described as a "voice" or "presence" that asks whether the person wants to return to life. The aftereffects of this "core experience" are dramatic and profound. As described in *"Life at Death,"* the fear of death tends to vanish and the total impact is akin to a spiritual rebirth. The conclusions Dr. Ring has reached are very dramatic when one considers that they are coming from a man of science who does not dare reach conclusions until he has tallied up all the evidence.

"I do believe – but not just on the basis of my own or others' data regarding near-death-experience – that we continue to have a conscious existence after our physical death and that the core experience does represent its beginning, a sort of glimpse of things to come. I am, in fact, convinced – both from my own personal experiences and from my studies as a psychologist – that it is possible to become conscious of 'other realities' and that the coming close to death represents one avenue to a higher 'frequency domain,' or reality, which will be fully accessible to us following what we call death."

As far as Dr. Ring is concerned, the near-death-experience is important not only to the person who has undergone it. He sees a far more important implication in such experiences, experiences which he feels are meant to have a profound impact on society as a whole.

"My own understanding of these near-death-experiences leads me to regard them as 'teachings.' They are, it seems to me, by their nature, revelatory experiences. They vouchsafe both to those who undergo them and to those who hear about them an intuitive sense of the transcendent aspect of creation. These experiences clearly imply that there is something more, something beyond the physical world of the senses, which, in the light of these experiences, now appears to be only the mundane segment of a greater spectrum of reality."

And why are such experiences seemingly increasing in number at this time in our history? Dr. Ring has a speculative answer which can be justified in light of some other theories that will be discussed later on in this book.

"I have come to believe," states the astute author, "that the universe has many ways of 'getting its message across.' In a sense, it wants us to 'wake up,' to become aware of the cosmic dimensions of the drama of which we are all a part. Near-death-experiences represent one of its devices for waking us up to this higher reality. The 'message' – for the experiencing individual at least – is usually so clear, potent, and undeniable that it is neither forgotten nor dismissed. Potentially, then, those who have these experiences become 'prophets' to the rest of us who have fallen back to sleep or have never been awakened. From this point of view, the voices we have heard are those of prophets preaching a religion of universal brotherhood and love and of divine compassion. This, obviously, is no new message; it acquires its significance chiefly from the unusual experiential circumstances that give rise to it – the state of consciousness associated with the onset of apparent death."

In his book, Dr. Ring refers to these near-death episodes as "seed experiences," and in a sense they are no different than the UFO encounters of the third kind that many people have been experiencing in growing numbers in that they represent not only an actual physical experience for the person involved, but are a symbol to the rest of humankind that it is time our consciousness be expanded into other realms and dimensions . . . which is, after all, what all our work and writings are about!

Similar research has been conducted by Dr. Michael B. Sabom, Assistant Professor of Medicine, Division of Cardiology at Emory University, and a staff physician at the Atlanta VA Medical Center. Dr. Sabom began his internship at the University of Florida in July, 1970, and, as he had been trained in scientific methodology, he was not quick to consider talk of life after death and the supposed experiences of several patients who had reportedly returned from the gates of heaven.

But, little by little, as he worked with individuals who had undergone extreme heart problems, he began to realize that such near-death-experiences were more common than he had ever supposed and seemed to be quite similar in nature, no matter who they came from.

Harper & Row published Dr. Sabom's findings in 1981 under the title "Recollections of Death – A Medical Investigation." In this volume, the author tells of his findings and conclusions based on a personal study of 106 case histories.

"As a physician," Sabom writes, "I have evaluated the medical circumstances that have surrounded these experiences and have been utterly amazed at the survival of many of these people whose physical condition plainly seemed to rule against their continuing to live. I have been equally fascinated by the descriptions of their journeys while unconscious and near death. My personal reaction to these events is not so much a 'scientifically weighed' response as it is a keenly felt identification with the tears of joy and sorrow that have accompanied the unfolding of many of these stories."

As to what these experiences "mean," Dr. Sabom quotes the words of one of his patients who returned from the dead: "I think it's God's work. That's the only thing I can figure. God had me that time and He could have kept me. From this experience, I know there is a life after death and not just death itself. I think once you've penetrated the big secret just a bit like I did, it's enough to convince you, enough to convince me that I'm going to have no fear . . . I don't think God wanted me to die . . . If He wanted me, He would have kept me . . . He wanted me to get a peek into this big secret and shove me right back again."

CLERGYMAN EXPLAINS: "WHY I BELIEVE."

And what of the clergy? While life after death may have been an accepted doctrine in decades past, a good number of "modern" theologians subscribe to the theory that, when the body dies, that's it for all eternity. Or at least you're going to remain "in the ground" until the time when Jesus returns and personally lifts our souls up from the grave and either sends them to heaven or straight to hell. However, little by little, this "dark ages" approach to a very important subject is being radically disputed by men of the cloth who are willing to study all the evidence and make up their own mind based both upon the scriptures of the Bible (which tells us the soul does live on in other dimensions) or by discussing the topic with members of their congregation who might even have been – at least momentarily – closer to God than they've ever been.

One such clergyman is the Rev. R. E. Allten, whose writing on the subject of survival became his Master of Sacred Theology thesis to Harvard University. The Rev. Allten originally submitted his thesis to "Chimes," a now-defunct publication which contained frequent accounts of those who had experienced physical death. Rev. Allten's thinking on the topic is clear and concise and is typical of the rationale now being employed by ministers and priests whose bound duty it is to proclaim the existence of God's higher kingdoms.

"It all began on a hot summer afternoon in 1952. I had just served the Sacrament of Holy Communion to Mr. Thurston Wiggin of East Corinth, Maine, who was dying of the dreaded disease, leukemia. Mr. Wiggin had been ill for some time. My predecessor in the Methodist Pastorate at this little rural town in north central Maine had called faithfully at Mr. Wiggin's home for many months in an effort to bring him the comfort of the Christian faith. After my transfer to the parish, I had continued to make frequent visits to the Wiggin home for the purpose of bringing peace of heart and mind to this valiant man who had been putting up such a courageous battle against the onslaughts of the black angel of death.

"As the months wore on, however, the dying man came to realize that his was a losing battle; he began to reconcile himself to the fact that it would not be too long before the final curtain would ring down upon the last act of his physical life on earth. He requested that I bring the Lord's Supper to his bedside so that he could experience one last hour of fellowship with Christ before the deepening shadows completely closed him off from his awareness of earthly existence.

"After he had received the bread and wine, he closed his eyes; his head sank back onto the pillow and he breathed a sigh of great relief. His face seemed to be more relaxed and peaceful than I had remembered seeing it in all the time I had been ministering to him. I knew that he had made his peace with God.

"As I rose to make my exit from the sick room, Mr. Wiggin turned his head toward me, opened his eyes, and said in a weak voice, 'I don't suppose I'll be here too much longer. My loved ones on the other side were all here last night. They waved to me and said, "Thurston, you'll be seeing us again soon. We are coming to take you home. Helen also will be joining us before too long."' Fortunately, his wife, Helen, had been out of the room and did not hear the last part of this statement. I quickly leaned over the bed and said to him, 'We hope that you were only dreaming. You'll be around for quite a while yet, so don't take this experience too seriously.'

"Young pastors, in their zeal to bring immediate comfort, sometimes make brash statements; this was one of my unforgettable false messages of hope. I shall never forget its resultant effect. A strange look came over Mr. Wiggin's face as he struggled to frame the words, 'It was no dream, Pastor Allten. I was wide awake at the time. I saw those people and they were as real as you are. Don't you believe,' he said, 'in angels and in the life beyond the grave?'

"I hastily assured him that I did believe in life eternal and then sputtered something about remembering him in my prayers. I made a very rapid exit. As I drove back to the parsonage, I thought to myself how unfortunate it was that drugs and opiates had to be used in such quantities to deaden physical pain that the mind became delirious and thought processes distorted. I found a small measure of comfort, however, in the fact that at least the human brain had a way of softening the blow of imminent death, and that God in His mercy had so structured the mind that it was able to cope with any unbearable situation.

"Less than a week later, I committed Thurston Wiggin's physical body to our 'Holy Mother, the earth' in a simple ceremony which was held at the beautiful little Corinthian Cemetery, which overlooks the rolling hills and green pastures of the sleepy little village of East Corinth, where Mr. Wiggin had spent the greater part of his earthly life. His wife, Helen, wept quietly as I intoned the final words of the benediction. She left the grave with the words, 'I'm glad that his suffering is over and that he is now at home with the Lord.'

"'Yes,' I thought to myself, 'had he lived on too much longer he might have lost his mind completely; it would have been a horrible thing. As it was, he died quietly with full confidence in a beautiful illusion.'

"I walked slowly past the graves of those who had been dead for years, stopping only once to look at a gravestone on which was sculptured the image of an angel. I went through the iron gates of the cemetery and back to the land of the living.

"I called on Helen Wiggin two or three times after that. She seemed to be adjusting satisfactorily to her new life. Her grief was intense, but she showed every indication of being able to conquer it in the due course of time. She was in good health, had a nice family of grown children, and was qualified to teach school and was thus able to earn a comfortable living. I soon turned my attentions to others who seemed to be in more urgent need of my pastoral services. Life rolled on, as it always does. I moved to another student parish and the Wiggin family passed into the pastoral care of another student shepherd.

"About two years later, Helen Wiggin died on the operating table; she had succumbed to a routine surgical operation from which everyone had expected her to recover. I was stunned when I was informed of her passing. The prophetic words of her dead husband's revelators had come true. 'Helen will be joining us soon,' they had said. Her untimely death seemed to me to be more than a coincidence."

MEETING YOUR MAKER

Lori C. is a spiritually oriented person who has studied UFO literature, Star People concepts and New Age work in general. She is also an active wife and mother, a happy, cheerful person who practices good metaphysical beliefs in her everyday life and who makes them work for her both in the daily dimension and in contacting higher levels of consciousness.

Before a near-fatal auto accident, however, Lori was unhappy, unfulfilled – virtually another person, according to her friends and family as well as in her own conception of her personality. "I am truly another person," she states. "I remember immediately after the impact, I was laying in this twisted mass of metal which had been my sports car – dying for all intents and purposes."

Lori shakes her attractive blonde head and tears come to her eyes. "All I felt was utter serenity and peace. Then I began zapping my full power of concentration – my full being, if you will – to a magnificent light in the distance. It was pulsing and shimmering. To go to this beautiful, alive light, I had to sail through a dimly lit tunnel. Its walls were pulsing also, with less-intense energy, as if it was an extension of the focal-point light."

At this point, Lori indicates that "light" should truly be spelled with a capital "L" because this was truly the Cosmic God, the Life-force itself!

"I knew unequivocally and eternally at that very moment that there is life after death! It was as plain as the simplest fact – plainer than ABC had been when I was 6 years old. Death was, as far as I was concerned, only a passageway to a higher level of consciousness! This other level – other world – I saw so briefly was free of all the worries and hassles that we have here on this level. And yet, this level we're on now is a necessary one! Don't make the mistake of thinking that it is inferior or all bad because it is not! We have definite missions to do here – all of us in the human race do – to make this level a better, more Godly place to live!

"So I did see the other side. There IS another side and it is a beautiful place! But then, right as I was sailing through this pulsating tunnel, almost to the Light, I

71

was pulled back very abruptly. I was being put in the ambulance back here. I felt very sad . . . very sad . . . to be pulled away from the Light, but I understood that I had work left to do here and that I had not been doing it as I should have been before the accident. I made a vow to the Light and all the beings of the Higher Realms right then and there to carry forth my earth mission in a more diligent and loving kind of way. I vowed to start by treating my family with the overt love which I felt for them deep inside myself anyway. I just had not been showing it!

"I became more tolerant, more giving, more unconditionally loving not only with my family but with all life everywhere."

At this point, Lori's husband chimes in to say that she still seems to him like a totally different person, "Now she is a truly illuminated soul, 'a light shining for us all,' guiding us daily. Before she was petty, grudging, edgy."

Lori laughs lightly and her husband moves over to take her hand, "Oh, I loved her anyway," he smiles, "and I was and am no saint myself. But she underwent some wonderful kind of metamorphosis or transformation. I could never say that I'm glad the accident happened, but I do thank my lucky stars, and, to use Lori's term, I do thank the God-force that she is who she is today, right now, at this very minute!"

Today Lori does spiritual counseling, helping others to perceive and reach for higher levels of consciousness without their having to go through a near-death-experience. She is devoting full time to her mission and doing it well, making many people "new" again and enthusiastic about life itself. She is so certain about her visit to the world which lies waiting after death that she transfuses this absolute belief and reassurance into other people. We can only say, "Lori, carry on your mission!"

EXPERIENCING A SOUL ENCOUNTER

When we look at Lori's case with our psychic intuition, we know that she is indeed a blessed and inspired person. She encountered another dimension which touched her profoundly and deeply – right to her soul. In fact, it was her soul itself which experienced and remembers this near-death phenomenon. This is the only way to account for the basic personality changes within her! It was not her brain nor her physical body which changed but instead the unique essence which is Lori: it was enhanced, energized and recharged with goodness before its return to the mundane plane to engage in its life mission. She had been put off her "star path" by several paces, involved in self and negativism. Now Lori truly perceives what life is, how sacred and precious . . . and how eternal.

Lori truly had a soul encounter with higher beings! Lori also states that she feels close to her "special one," a guardian angel. Before the accident, she had barely suspected that such a being might exist but she had no real communication or contact with this being. However, these days Lori communes with her special spirit guide daily, and he gives her strength and assistance in making the right, loving choices and in guiding others. He transmits to Lori the message that there is no death, and that his soul, her soul – and your soul, dear reader – have been within the Universal Energy for millennia upon millennia. They come from the Universal Energy and they are the Universal Energy!

Death in this one lifetime certainly does not mean death of this unique, vital, and ageless energy essence called the soul. It shall never die, only evolve on to brave new worlds, on to breathtaking new dimensions.

MORE PROOF OF HEAVENLY REALMS
–THE WHITE LIGHT AND CELESTIAL MUSIC

As fascinating as Lori's experience may be to us, it is within keeping with other similar "after death" episodes that have been reported to us. Take, for example, the case of attorney Robert D., who should have died during the Second World War but who is still around today thanks to that "invisible hand" that often saves lives in the nick of time, even when it becomes most unlikely.

"My near-death-experience happened in 1944 while I was an enlisted bombardier-navigator in a medium bomber group stationed on Sardinia," Robert began, going into detail about experiencing the "white light" so many soul travelers have spoken of as well as hearing strange music which can only be described as purely "celestial."

"My group's mission on the day involved was to bomb a German marshalling area at a small city near the Adriatic, the name of which I can't recall. We were told at briefing the importance of the target and that it would be 'flacked up,' a kind of 'last letter home' mission. It was a clear summer day with ceiling and visibility unlimited (CAW weather). This must have been about my 26th or 27th mission, although, with the lapse of years, I forget that, too. It really isn't important, except that it denotes that I had by then had a good bit of combat experience.

"We turned on an IP (Indicated Point) perhaps 6-5 miles west of the target area and began flying east. It was about 10:30 or 11 AM and the sun was bright overhead. It was so hot in my 'greenhouse' that I took off my leather flying jacket. In our B-26 aircraft, the bombardier had the best view on the aircraft, as you were out in a Plexiglas nose with unobstructed vision.

"As we came closer to the target, I could see flack so thick that the stuff looked like a coal pile over the city. Earlier medium bomber formations were already bombing the area and as I watched I saw bomber after bomber shot down out there in front of us. By a rough guess, I would imagine I was observing a loss ratio of about 65% of the total formations' strength.

"It was procedure for the bombardier to keep his intercom on 'local' or within plane during a bomb run, so as to communicate with the pilot and guide the plane right or left as you bombed. Usually the co-pilot kept his radio on command channel so that he could hear the group leader's instructions.

"As I watched the bombers in the flack being shot down, I suddenly realized that most likely I would be dead in the next few minutes.

"I was then an agnostic. I always said that if I was about to die I would not get 'foxhole religion.' Recognizing death approaching I still did the automatic things a good bombardier should do on approach. I turned on the intervelometer, armed the bombs and prepared to open bomb bay doors, all the time gritting my 20 year old teeth and saying, 'There is no God and I won't change my belief now.'

"It is taking much longer to type this than the actual time involved. Perhaps the whole thing lasted 3 minutes, maybe one. But, at any rate, my earphones suddenly were filled with music when previously there had been static. It was indescribably beautiful. You could say it sounded like organs, a full symphony orchestra, violins, or any musical instrument you ever heard. It was almost too low to hear initially but built to a crescendo of sound . . . something a bit like church music or classical music but about impossible to describe. And as the music enveloped me, I was conscious of being the center of a very white light. This light, however, gave off no heat and was separate from the sunlight flooding the nacelle. It seems (remembering) that the light extended out from me in any direction 30 to 40 feet.

"I remember thinking, 'So this is how it is to die!' The combination of music and light produced in me a feeling of euphoria absolutely impossible to adequately describe, even though I'm remembering it very clearly some 32 years or so later and trying my best to be explicit.

"At the time, the music was more enveloping than what I was accustomed to hearing from the earphones and radio. As a boy, I sat by our church organist as she played, and my skin felt the big vibrations of notes from the pipes. Recalling, I think that I was hearing the music and sensing the light from an inner reality not connected with physical life because the experience was much more vivid than any externally received music (before or since), no matter whether sitting near a pipe organ, in an orchestra, or listening to my current stereo system at home. (College orchestra 2 years before.)

"And I must emphasize that I knew I was about to die on that bomb run. It was as if every molecule in my body was boiling with its individual knowledge

74

that the physical entity of me was about to cease except for small slivers of bone, skin, blood to drift down to the ground. In such a heightened state of awareness, just maybe I heard the music and saw the light which may exist in the next dimension(s), because I momentarily 'shifted gears' and could perceive from the 'in' outwardly rather than our customary intake of sensory perception of physical reality.

"The total experience must have been brief. It was over when our formation banked left and turned in a northerly direction to hit a secondary target which proved to be a 'milk run.' I called the pilot on intercom and asked why we were banking. He explained that the group commander in our lead plane had decided not to hit the primary but to go bomb a secondary target to the north (This heard over command channel).

"When we landed, I asked the pilot and co-pilot if they had heard the music and seen the light on the initial bomb run. They gave me funny looks and said they hadn't. Afterwards, they refused to fly with me, and I was informally grounded in the squadron for about 3 or 4 weeks, with no explanation given.

"After that mission, I quit being the squadron agnostic-in-residence in bull sessions simply because I concluded I didn't know all there was to know about death and an afterlife, and that God had opened the door to heaven briefly for me.

"That is my psychic experience from WW II. Today, I rarely talk about combat and certainly not that experience. The biggest tragedy of my life (looking back at 53) was 40 missions and a lot of killing of men, women and children. At the time, I was truly a war lover; a volunteer from Tennessee, anxious to go kill Germans. I'm a different person today than that young man in a bomber. This near death episode taught me a lot and changed my life for the better. I'm convinced I was being shown what to expect when I die. I saw the white light and heard the eerie celestial music – I'm convinced heaven must exist!"

The third case we wish to take a look at concerns a man named Lee who had been involved with a life after death experience; not his own but his brother, Bob's. Unlike Lori, Lee is uneducated, both in book-learning and in metaphysics and spiritualism. Lee is a man of the soil, of the earth. He is a good but simple man, living in rural Tennessee all his life. He has been to Nashville but that is the extent of his travel. However, he is a wise soul and a much-valued life form in the cosmic scheme of things.

NO MORE PHYSICAL PAIN

Lee watched his brother Bob die slowly of cancer. "It took ten months," sighs Lee, "and it wasn't a pretty thing to watch." Lee took care of Bob very carefully, helping with all details from personal hygiene to funeral arrangements. The two became even closer than they had been earlier in life; a link was formed psychically.

"Bob told me that if he possibly could, he would get through from heaven – from that other world – and let me know that there is life after death because he thought (and I did, too) that that would be the biggest darn gift he could give me. We thought it was the best 'thanks' in the whole world to just really get the information back through from the other side to the person waiting here on earth. To absolutely have that knowledge . . . would be the greatest thing!

"Well, Bob died early one Sunday morning, you know. It was raining cats and dogs, very gloomy. I called the parson at the funeral home. There was no one else here and I did the whole thing. I did it even though I was grieving and crying. Bob held my hand as he took his last breath, so I was struggling with that having happened – to actually have been there at the moment – plus all the worries that went with it afterward. Well, I thank you, I had just about had it. That Sunday afternoon, I sat down on the sofa and just started to sob. Neither Bob nor I had any other living soul in the universe that we were close to and now I felt that we were parted . . . that he was as lonely in some cold strange new world as I was here on earth. Suddenly, as I sat there, I stopped my sobbing because a really nice warm wave washed over me, almost like being bathed with warm water. I looked over by the fireplace there and I saw Bob. I swear on my life that I really did see him; it was no illusion just because I was so tired."

Lee continues telling his story with tears welling in his eyes. "You know, it was Bob as he had looked one, maybe two years before his death. He did not have all those horrible things wrong with him that the cancer had done. He looked young and happy and full of joy. He was a whole figure – not just a head or something like in ghost stories – and he was looking right at me! Then, I swear by all that is holy, he nodded his head real strongly, just once, and I knew in my bones that he was saying, 'Yes, there is life after death. I am in that heavenly other world and it is just grand here. Just lovely.'

"Then after that one strong nod, as if saying, 'Yep,' he faded out right before my eyes. He just winked out and was gone.

"I swear, I wouldn't believe it if anyone else told me. But this happened to me, doggone it, and I know what I saw and I know what I felt. I also know what I now firmly believe that there is life after death in a very good world where there are no wars, no fights, no hatred and meanness!"

After examining Lee's case closely, we find that he and his brother had formed a very real and lasting cosmic bond. Their energies washed together and merged as one consciousness, thus making Bob's visit back from the other world an easier thing to accomplish. In other words, had the two not been so close, Bob might have only been able to appear for a second as a mere blur, but since there was their duality of life energy present, Bob was able to appear in full and give a very obvious, concise message. And we must remember what his message was, for this is the most important message within the pages of this book: There Is Life After Death!

"I KNOW MY BLIND GRANDMOTHER CAN SEE IN THE AFTERLIFE"

In the second issue of "Inner Light," I told a fascinating first-person story which is worthy of repeating now since that particular issue was only sent to a limited mailing list in those days. Christine Colby is a dear friend of mine. For five years, we both taught first grade in a St. Petersburg, Florida, elementary school. Chris was always a devoted teacher. She was loving and caring, yet capable of discipline as well as guidance. She has always been a very sensitive and spiritual woman. Throughout her life, Chris had been exceptionally close to her paternal grandmother. She feels they might even have known each other in a past life. In addition, they were able to communicate with each other even though they might be separated by distance.

"When I was sick or distressed, Grandmother Petricelli would call on the phone or arrive at my side without having to be asked," Chris told me. "My Grandmother might have been blind, but her mental capabilities were so keen that they gave her an inner sight which was overwhelmingly beautiful. When Grandmother died, I knew I had not only lost a dear relative but also a best friend and twin soul."

Chris revealed during the course of one conversation that when her granny died she felt all alone. "It was 1975, I was just 18 years old and had not yet met my husband. I was really devastated. Frankly, while I love my mother a lot, she and I have never had a natural bond nor have we always seen eye to eye on everything. Thus losing my grandmother was like losing a part of my soul.

"Grandmother died early on the morning of August 18th," Chris sighed. "By that night, my parents had taken care of the details of her funeral. My parents, my sister and I were staying at my grandmother's house. We were all physically and emotionally exhausted after a terribly long and hard day. I felt that I should spend the night in Grandmother's room, whereas my sister, who had not been that close to her, said she was too scared to stay in a room where a person had just died.

"I, on the other hand, welcomed this last chance to be near Grandmother if only in spirit. I could still smell the good perfume on the pillow and I appreciated the little belongings that were hers and had not yet been packed away. I looked at the friendly little room and thought how much Grandmother had hated being blind those five years before her death. She particularly loved nature and bright colors and had often expressed to me how sad she was not to be able to see anymore."

My friend's warm, brown eyes filled with tears as she relived this amazing night. "My sister was teasing me that I should leave the light on all night, that grandmother's ghost might come and haunt me. Actually, I didn't think she was being funny at all. There was nothing for me to be scared of. I had loved my Grandmother. She was a good soul and the darkness in what had been her private place was a very peaceful thing to me. I'm mentioning my sister being a tease to you because it's very important. You see, because of her I'm certain I turned off the lights in that room before I went to sleep. I remember lying there in the darkness, thinking that this was the black world Grandmother had lived in. And yet I still felt very warm and safe there in her bed."

Eventually, Chris fell asleep in the darkness. "In the middle of the night, when I had been asleep for some time, I heard someone calling my name. I opened my eyes and was immediately aware that the light was on in the bedroom. The voice I was hearing was my mother calling to me wanting to know if I was okay and why didn't I finally turn off the light and go to sleep. I replied that I had been asleep and that I had turned the light off hours ago. My mother could hear that my voice was getting excited and she came to the door, asking if I'd please let her in. You see, I had locked the door before going to sleep, just to make myself feel secure within my Grandmother's room and so that my sister wouldn't come back in and tease me.

"The reason my voice was getting so excited was that I absolutely knew why the light was on. I knew that Grandmother had turned the light on in the room! I also understood the message she was trying to get across to me. Her message was that she once again had light, she once again could see . . . that she was free of the blindness and death that had claimed her."

Chris' account is truly a thrilling one. It not only offers proof that her grandmother's soul survived and that the spirit could communicate with the living person with whom it had felt closest, but that the soul could send back an intelligent, loving message. Chris' communications with her grandmother continued for a week after her passing. Always the message was clear: "I am alive, I can see, it is very beautiful where I am!"

The final message came a week to the day after her grandmother's death. Chris was shopping in a crowded department store, just leaving the section which displays pocketbooks and purses. At the far end of this large area, Chris' gaze fell on a plain brown purse which was hung against the wall many feet away. There was nothing remarkable about the purse. Nonetheless, she felt compelled to go over to it and turn it around. There, on the other side of the purse, was an embroidered petti-point scene of a woodland meadow. Chris' heart thumped with excitement and she recalls with joy the feelings that swept over her on this occasion.

"That scene was the same exact one Grandmother had embroidered for me on a pillow before she went blind. I mean, it was exactly the same! The purse had been accidentally turned to the wall so that the embroidered side could not be seen at all. Still, I was absolutely, and mysteriously, compelled to go way across the room to that plain brown purse and turn it around. In my mind and my soul, I knew that Grandma was saying, 'Goodbye. I must now go to the peaceful, beautiful land much like this one. I just want to let you know I am alive and joyous beyond words.'

"After this experience, I did not hear from her regularly again and I knew that she had passed on to her lovely new world."

However, Chris did hear from her grandmother on one more occasion . . . an occasion which was very important in Chris' life. Chris and her husband had tried hard to have a family, but the doctors told them it would be impossible. Immediately, they started adoption proceedings, but the red tape was frustrating and costly. The wait to get their baby was a long one and Chris became extremely depressed. "I just sat down one day and cried my eyes out," she remembers. "I had no one to turn to but my beloved grandmother. So I turned my tear-filled eyes upward and asked her to help me, to give me a sign as to whether we'd get our baby.

"After I had dried my eyes, I felt compelled to go to my jewelry box and there, right on the top, was my grandmother's class ring which was very old and very dear to me but had been lost since before her death. I had been afraid to tell her about this as I didn't want to hurt her feelings. I couldn't believe my eyes as I gazed at that ring because I had looked in my jewelry box many times over the years. There is no way that the ring could have been there all along. It was an absolute miracle, and I knew it was Grandmother's way of telling me very soon that I would get my baby."

Sure enough, Chris did adopt a child. And so, on that lovely note, my friend's dramatic proof of life after death draws to a close. There can be no other explanation, for the events that happened to Chris showed that her grandmother truly did conquer death and achieved freedom from physical ailments and emotional worries, transcending to a peaceful and magnificent spiritual meadowland which some of us call Heaven.

HEAVEN IS WHAT YOU MAKE IT

In my spiritual and psychic education in this lifetime, my guides have shown me that each mind/soul makes its own reality, both while here on earth and also in the afterlife. Your mind waves are unique unto themselves and they do create the reality which you see around you. Your reality is a hologram created by your mind/soul. Therefore, when you die, you also create the reality to which you will go. Yes, it exists on its own as well . . . but your mind/soul cannot find its frequency unless it is tuned in. This is like being tuned into a radio station: you simply cannot hear it unless you hit the right spot on the frequency dial. Therefore, you tune into a reality as you leave this corporeal life. It is basically your choice!

STANDING AT THE DOOR OF CREATION

Jesus said, "I stand at the door and knock." He meant that one can find the Christed reality of goodness (heaven) if one is of good heart and soul. You need not have lived a perfect, sinless life; you need only tune into the higher consciousness frequency in order to arrive, upon physical death, at a bright new dimension which can indeed be called the heavenly dimension. And so your afterlife stands at the door and knocks.

In a very real sense, you may choose a world which is of the Eastern tradition of Nirvana and ecstatic mind experience. Or, your mind may be involved with the pure Christian beliefs, in which case you can and will find Jesus and the heavenly hosts in all their glory. If you are a starward-bound mind/soul, you will indeed find yourself traveling the stars and exploring new, higher worlds/planets which are now out of your reach. A warning, however: if you are obsessed with negativism, with worrying about Satanic influence, with carrying on hatred of your fellow man or of another individual, then your mind/soul is creating even now an afterlife which is not heaven at all. We must not preoccupy ourselves in judging or condemning others, for then we do not tend to the beautiful garden of energy which is our own uniqueness, our own soul.

You do choose the world to which you will go. You are choosing it in your everyday actions and deeds even now. You must stay in the positive flow and you must be of goodness and good intent! Have no doubts that there is indeed life after death waiting for your soul, which lives forever.

REINCARNATION

In your next life, you may or may not have memories of this life. If you believe in reincarnation, then you will live another life as a human here on earth or out in the cosmos, for that is the reality you make for your eternal mind/soul. When you do live another life on earth or another planet, if you explore your sub-consciousness and your supra-consciousness enough, you will find memories of the life you are living now. It is and will be recorded in your mind-waves for all eternity. The experiences you now have are stored as a computer would store facts, within that unique energy which is you! I do not talk here of your brain, for all brains look very similar under a microscope. No, I am speaking of your mind and your soul, which cannot be explored under a microscope but which are the most precious possessions you own! The mind/soul points you along your star path of life; it remembers cosmically; it guides with the beautiful God-wisdom which it possesses, for it is a part of the God-force. It is life. It is life eternal!

I cherish each and every one of the thousands of letters I have received which ask about life after death and which confirm life after death. The question is every bit as important as the answer . . . for the question makes the answer a universal truth! In other words, in reading this book, you, dear reader, are expressing curiosity about life after death. You are opening your mind/soul to the possibility of it and you are beginning to choose what dimensional frequency you want to reach after death of your physical body.

In this curiosity you are expressing you are, at this very second, engineering a bright new heavenly reality for yourself after death. That reality cannot exist unless your mind/soul reaches out to it as it is at this moment. You cannot find the right spot on the dial if you don't first turn the dial!

That is exactly the way it is with questions and answers about life after death: Once you start to reach out and to search, you do find the right spot on your dial eventually. However, if you do not make that original move to change the dial, you are stuck on "nonexistence." If you don't question, if you don't reach out, if you become stagnant and non-changing, then you do face the only real death of mind/soul. If you change, reach out, explore . . . then you live both in this life and in all lives to come. They do lie ahead on your star path, do not doubt this! Life is change. Death is transition. They are one in the same. All is life.

Actress Ida Lapino claims to have received a phone call from the world of the dearly departed.

WHEN IT BECOMES YOUR TURN TO DIE

Death is a scary subject. Many of us refuse to discuss our innermost thoughts on the matter even with the ones we love. It is something forbidden, dark, mysterious, and just too plain ugly to be taken seriously – until it is often too late. How frequently have we seen a loved one near death's door with a lot pressing on their mind, and yet, no matter how close we are to that person, we cannot bring ourselves to talk about an issue that is so obviously of immediate importance. Often in a hospital room or near a sick bed the tension is so thick that you can cut it with a knife.

But why are we so scared as we approach a situation that we must all come to grips with? Naturally, there is much sadness in knowing that a family member, a loved one, or a close friend is not going to be around much longer. However, there's something much more than just sadness that seems to freeze our veins as we find ourselves confronted with the grim reaper face to face. What we are most afraid of is the great unknown. We are apprehensive about what lives around the next corner. Luckily, there is much we can do to comfort the ill at ease and to make the transition a lot easier on those who are uncomfortable with death.

There are now a handful of organizations that are helping to alleviate the suffering of those who are about to die as well as the loved ones of those who are about to pass over. One such organization is the Metascience Foundation (Box 747, Franklin, N.C. 28734) headed by George Meek, an expert in electronic voice phenomenon and inventor of the Spiritcom, an electronic device described in another chapter which has successfully been used to communicate with departed souls who now reside on other spiritual planes close to the earth's physical surface.

Some of the literature issued by the Metascience Foundation has actually been transmitted across the heavens from spirit beings who once resided right here on our world.

"As We See It From Here" is one such volume which comes to us via the late Dr. Jesse Herman Holmes, a leading Quaker who for twenty-five years was head

of the Department of Religion and Philosophy at Swarthmore College. Dr. Holmes, who died in 1942, has apparently been lending assistance from the spirit world along with a team of well-known writers, philosophers, artists, theologians and poets who have "come back" to tell us what it is like on the other side as well as to assure us that life continues even after we have shed our present shell of a body.

One of the areas Dr. Jesse Herman Holmes and his "spirit staff" seem most interested in is the dignity of death and ways in which the transition can be made the easiest for everyone concerned.

"There are ways in which people can be helped while still in the physical body," affirms the departed theologian. "Too many times the aged, the infirm, the institutionalized are left alone and struggle to be rid of the physical at the bidding of those energies of light and love which they see about them. Too many leave this world during such struggles. But there are ways that assistance can be given. If those in the older years could have some instruction in the ways of self-help, it would be well for them. Unfortunately, society today seems interested only in ways and means pertinent to the material life. Even the churches which many attend throughout their lifetimes, although giving much opportunity for building helpful thought-forms, offer no practical instruction in the ways of leaving (behind) the body."

"As We See It From Here" continues by telling the precise way in which the soul departs from the body. "Ordinarily the spirit withdraws after that period in which the mind turns inward, shutting out the material world. The spirit then begins its withdrawal upward, beginning at the lower extremities. This upward passage is a doubling or condensing of those energies of which the human spirit consists. It rolls upward from the lower extremities, and, passing through the long length of the body, it enters what was called by the ancients the 'Kingdom of Heaven through the narrow way,' the small passage at the top of the head which is softer and less dense than other portions of the physical skull. It is the way in which the spirit enters the newly prepared body at the beginning of life. It is the way in which the spirit leaves the aged, infirm and physically insufficient body at the end of life."

The authors find this description extremely fascinating because in several instances that we have personally investigated those who told about dying described how they felt each and every cell in their body start to go numb and die. The sensation, they told us, started at the tip of their toes and worked its way up the body until it felt like their brain was about to collapse in on itself.

According to Dr. Holmes (or should we say his spirit), as this transition starts to take place, the eyes of the dying roll up and they become sensitive to the energies around them. "The mental screen becomes illuminated at the last breath or two, and the person catches a slight glimpse of surrounding astral areas and the lights. These lights maintain more or less the appearance or form of bodies, hence can be recognized by the departing spirit as those who have gone on or who have been near and dear and who now reside in other dimensions."

As life's last glimmer passes before us, there is, says Dr. Holmes, a way in which we can perfect and make easier the passing away of the body. "When the individual approaching death feels the coldness of lower extremities of the body, he should breathe deeply, evenly, calmly, with the eyes shut, and let the consciousness reach upward, feel the upward tug, the tug of the upper levels of the spirit towards the narrow way through which it will escape the body. To be completely relaxed, to breathe deeply, evenly and to resist not the upward tug of the spirit is the way of self-help for the individual.

"An eager anticipation of this experience with the fire and enthusiasm of ideals is the best self-help that one can have. When one has prepared in this fashion, the demons of fear are exorcised and banished from one's being. There is only love, anticipation, and eagerness to step through the door into other dimensions – a most beautiful experience!"

HOW TO DIE

Is there, indeed, a right or a wrong way in which to die? Probably one of the best papers ever issued on this subject was written by a nurse named Mabel Rowland. It was originally published in 1942 as a 24-page booklet and sold widely for 25¢. The copyright expired recently, and the paper has been kept in circulation by the above mentioned Metascience Foundation. We reprint it here since it is potentially important to all of us who will have to confront death sooner or later.

Regardless of who we are or how we feel about it, each one of us must one day leave the body. But there is absolutely no reason to fear this change, for LIFE is continuous, and, what is still more comforting, CONSCIOUSNESS and individuality are continuous. What happens is that the soul leaves the body we now dwell in and starts anew in its next phase of existence, vibrating at a different rate. The change is as natural as breathing, and we should be as trusting and fearless concerning it as we are about breathing. There is nothing to fear any more than when we lie down to sleep for the night.

As God's creatures, we are PRIVILEGED to live LIFE, and this privilege includes Stewardship of a body! A body housing this dynamic, precious and most wonderful thing in the world – LIFE. We must take every care of the body but we are not to presume that we own it. We dwell in it; we do not own it. The Creator put us into these bodies "for the duration" of our earth lives, and we are to follow the first law of Nature and strictly observe "self-preservation."

We are to fight for our lives to the very last ditch and to protect our bodies to the very best of our ability. Even an insect does as much, instinctively. Painless as we know "dying" to be, IT is Nature's own process and is arrived at upon the Creator's exact moment scheduled for us in the great plan.

WHEN WILL IT BE FOR ME?

Forget it! It is none of our business, but preparing for LIFE afterward IS. It is only fair to yourself to take in these few facts which I shall give you and remember them. You may not believe them, nor do you need to, but it is necessary for you to read and remember them; that is the intelligent thing to do. Then, when you need the information, it will suddenly pop up out of your subconscious mind and be useful.

Now, when we have completed this cycle of our earth life and IT is over and finished, we awaken in the next state of our existence, discovering that our thought and feeling reactions are exactly the same as they always were! Remember that. You are YOU. There is no death. There is only a change of apparel, so to speak. You have shed the body, but your thoughts and feelings do not undergo any change in the passing out. However, you become quickly conscious of the fact that things OTHER than yourself are slightly, but definitely, different and it is for THAT VERY REASON I am discussing this. So please heed this, that you may not be at all PAN-ICKY but know exactly what to do.

You probably at some time have dreamed you were falling. If so, you know that the dreamer never hits and hurts himself. He wakes up. In the experience of "dying," sometimes the individual realizes he is going, or he may merely suspect it, but the truth is, while people rarely admit it, even to themselves, most of them FEAR it. There is no need to. There is no death; it is a misnomer. The TRUTH is that the actual passing out is not only painless, as I noted a few moments ago, but often beautiful; a NATURAL transition, never to be dreaded. We do not get whisked to a city with "golden streets" and see angels flying around. No.

If there is any such place, which was held out to us as "bait" to be "good" in the theologies we were raised on, then we are certainly not ready, in our present state of being, to take up residence there anyway.

The REAL of the person leaves the body very much as a butterfly leaves its old chrysalis. Many, many persons everywhere have seen this passing out. I have seen it myself. Ask any experienced nurse. She will probably tell you of seeing a vaporous cloud of ectoplasm – that's what it looks like to our human vision. It is the silver cord that holds us to our bodies. Everyone has it and here in our earth life it is never severed. But it stretches when we are asleep to let our souls or entities, the real of us, go from the body and experience dreams. Then it shortens again and comes back to the body. It holds "body and soul" together.

There might be four or five people present at a bedside when a soul passes out and maybe only one or two of them will have their human vision stepped up to the frequency even to see this much. Some of us have seen a great deal more. There IS no death. Now you understand that you are the same individual after you leave the body as before. No wings, no thrones, no crowns. You may be pleased with conditions or you may at first be a little disappointed. It just depends on what you have expected. For the first few days, everyone's fate is the same, whether saint or sinner, and, after that, there are spheres of life where you will belong and nothing can keep you out of your sphere. You are drawn into it by the LAW of attraction; that law which proves that like attracts like.

We will be with people of the same tastes and degree of spiritual interests as ourselves, just as we naturally gravitate to and choose suitable associates here. Individual reactions are just that, individual reactions. And there are some people who have lived a sheltered earth-life to a ripe old age, steeped in theological tradition and with fixed ideas about streets of gold, gates of pearl, harps and so forth. These good souls are oftentimes their own worst enemies, being stubbornly unwilling to adjust to anything even similar to their earth life conditions, although the next plane IS similar – surprisingly so.

Some people, through theological training, actually expect, when they realize they have "died," to find the streets made of gold. Certain it is that if they believed that literally while here, they will be of the same opinion still. Some theologies teach that, when we die, the body, soul and entire entity lie in the grave and sleep until the "Judgment Day."

Well, these dear souls actually believe that literally. And when helpers on the other side of life try to tell them they are the same John or Annie Smith they've always been, but that now their life is going to have a few changes in its working out, they are skeptical and react as they might to a bunco man at the county fair. Some folks of this persuasion insist on sleeping until "Gabriel" shall blow his horn. They often sleep for years. Let us consider now a soul just out of the physical body through a natural leisurely process. It is YOURSELF perhaps.

You are greeting your parents. How wonderful they look and they have been gone for years! They were quite old and a little bent when you last saw them in earth life. It used to grieve and tug at you a little to see them aging and failing. But here they are as lovely looking and as smiling and happy as you remember them when they were young and you were very young, just starting to school back in the little home town. Perhaps you are dreaming – something like this has happened to you before in dreams.

No, they were very brief and fleeting flashes, those dreams. This is real and enduring. Still, your parents aren't saying very much, and that is like a dream, too. But their gaze is fond and steady and they smile so reassuringly. It is real. And what a nice cool light feeling you have! They embrace you. It is real! Lovingly, they lead you off into their own circle or vibration where you will rest and talk.

Soon you will experience a lovely, drowsy, but very safe feeling, and, letting yourself go, will fall into a sleep of anywhere from three days or so to several weeks. Even the most spiritual personalities we have any record of remained and rested the first sixty hours or a few days in the Astral, then sometimes reappeared here on earth, briefly, before ascending into higher realms. The "dead" person doesn't feel nor act any differently for having "died," but adjustments have to be made, just as they have to be made here on earth. For instance, when summer is waning, we move in off the sleeping porch, wrap up a bit and get out our furs and make a hearth fire.

That is all there is to it; it is that simple. When you have slept for your few days or so after "dying" and wakened to start living in your new environment, you never sleep again. You rest as all do in the spiritual realms, but they do not sleep. The exception is those people I just mentioned, waiting for Gabriel. Please bear in mind that when the soul leaves the body it doesn't GO anywhere. The change, geographically, is no greater than you would experience in life if you walked from one room to another, from a darkened room into a lighted one or from a warm room onto a cool balcony.

Please realize also that while your body is to be protected and cherished, leaving it, in God's own time, is no more to be feared than is sliding out of your overcoat, letting it fall on a chair and walking away from it. And at first there is no consciousness of this "shedding," as it were, of the body of flesh. Our rate of vibration has changed, that is all. And the life we have entered is so very much like the earth life that the new arrival is often quite confused, particularly if he has been taught all his life to expect something different.

Should you ever experience the baffling sensation of walking up to your loved ones, embracing them, while they, completely unaware of your presence, walk THROUGH you, do not get panicky. Do the same as you should do in an earth emergency or any situation which you don't understand. We are told by the Psalmists (Ps. 46:10) to "Be Still." It matters not what your religious belief is, or whether you have any – that is perfect advice. Just be perfectly still within your own mind and lift your thought to your highest concept – whatever YOU think of as GOD.

Call to It or Him or breathe His name silently or aloud, just so it is from the heart, which it will be then – it will be YOU "as a little child" and IMMEDIATELY – even more quickly than I can tell you this, help comes. Pleasant, friendly aid and you are never in that "spot" again. The helper finds your relatives and loved ones for you. This is necessary when deaths occur accidentally and suddenly.

Remember what you are reading PLEASE. Simply raise your consciousness. It is your same old consciousness you know, to YOUR OWN HEAVENLY FATHER. Just say as much as "Father" and help will come. The Astral realm is organized. I repeat: you need not believe this that you are reading, but please remember it. In accidental death and in wartime it all happens so suddenly that the soul may be hurtled out of the body and stand amidst a hellish scene of disaster and destruction and see his own body lying there. It isn't a pleasant experience, but it is LIFE. Life is progressive. It blooms and fades and grows again and lifts us from sphere to sphere INDIVIDUALLY and according to each one's consciousness.

Stand still and pray. Death is a natural part of life. If your life here has been devoted to the accumulation of material things or to the making of money, to the extent that you have come to be steeped in it – to enjoy it, say, more than anything else – you are building up a hazard for yourself in the "next world." Be wise enough not to have your chief interest a material one like collecting or selling to make money, because when we leave the body we go where there is NO ECONOMIC standard. Money is not used.

You will be a fish out of water unless you have a hobby which is something less material, more intangible and important than buying and selling. Things "of the earth earthy" are just that. Be careful not to grow so fond of them as to be obsessed by them, for once we actually LOVE things or money, then we are in danger of being drawn and held by this earth vibration. Briefly, that would mean that we should, as a disembodied soul, yours or mine, after we had died, hang around others still in earth-life, whose tastes and activities are the same as ours used to be.

Our satisfaction would be merely vicarious. There are hordes of these pitiful earth-bound souls haunting clearing houses, counting houses and money markets and trade centers of all sorts. Also, we see the souls morally weak and depraved in drinking joints and low places. While you are still living your physical existence, realize that money is important to you merely for body comfort needs. This is temporary, so don't feed your soul to it. In the next plane, you see no "business as usual" sign. It is then that your artistic attainments may be enjoyed, and you will receive instruction for far more noble service than moneygrubbing. So, my advice is, to be prepared and to prepare while still living here.

Cultivate your SOUL SIDE. Learn to love and serve your fellow man. If it is not easy for you to love people, it can be an impersonal kind of love until you become a more loving creature. Cut down on the criticisms of others and magnify their desirable qualities. I mean just to yourself, as they start to "irritate" you when

89

you think of them. The way they walk or talk or some little fault. Forget that and refuse to see it.

The Hindu, when he passes another human soul, mutters "pronom," meaning "The God in me salutes the God (part) of you." I am not being sentimental. I am giving you the key to the situation of living, more fully, both here and now and AFTERWARD!

World wars have come from tiny little warring feelings in the individual HUMAN HEART. People are shocked at first to hear that, but it is true. Self-seeking people here on earth have competed, connived, monopolized and hated in their driving urge to control. To be top man; to get most; have most; regardless of how and inconsiderate of at whose cost. Yes, little wars of greed (called "Ambition") starting in the individual human heart, larger wars in families, cities and governments finally form the snowball which becomes a WORLD WAR!

The cure of war is peace and it, also, must start in the individual human heart, with the word "UNITY," or oneness, coming to fruition in deed as well. We are leaves of one tree. Children of the same Father. Coals of one fire. And we are each one endowed with the great solvent power of LOVE, which, if recognized and USED INDIVIDUALLY, would immediately start working to redeem the world.

Let us live with our thought upon God and, with this attitude of mind, we shall be living the right way – and then surely we will "die" the right way.

EXACTLY WHERE IS HEAVEN?

Heaven is like no place on earth as Dr. Dick, an eminent Scottish philosopher who lived more than a hundred years ago, must have realized when he penned the following words: "Oh, could we wing our way with the swiftness of a seraph, from sun to sun, and from world to world, until we had surveyed all the systems visible to the naked eye, which are only a mere speck in the map of the universe.

"Could we, at the same time, contemplate the glorious landscapes and scenes of grandeur that exist. Could we also mingle with the pure and exalted intelligences which people those resplendent abodes, and behold their humble and ardent adorations of their Almighty Maker, their benign and condescending deportment toward one another – each esteeming another better than himself – and all united in the bonds of the purest affection, without one haughty or discordant feeling – what indignation and astonishment would seize us on our return to this obscure corner of creation."

As we know, the vessel that we call our physical body is very transitory. We do die. The question before us has always been, is the mind and spirit within a person also transitory, or is the thing we call the soul something which retains its life force? And if in fact it does, then where does the mind/spirit find itself after the physical body has ceased to function and is no longer in existence? In the Christian religion, as well as many other faiths, after a person has died, supposedly, their spirit migrates to a sphere of existence where he or she is either rewarded or punished for deeds performed while on earth. Thus originates the concept of heaven and hell.

Modern Christian theology leads us more and more to believe that the dead are gathering dust and do not live on. Instead they are said to remain in the ground until "Judgment Day" when Jesus – surrounded by an army of angels – will descend from the clouds, slay the wicked and lift up with Him into heaven those who are worthy.

On the other hand, those who have been damned will fall into hell's fiery pit

91

of damnation where they will suffer for all eternity trying to stay out of reach of Satan's razor sharp pitchfork. Actually, this philosophy is a rather current one which got a foothold sometime during the fourteenth century. It is also contrary to what Jesus taught and what the scriptures have to say about the subject of survival.

According to all existing evidence, there is every reason to accept the idea that when we die our soul transports itself to a place, a region, or a level of consciousness that befits the way we lived while on earth. Heaven, dear friends, is not one single place but is a series of spiritual zones that are literally the way you believe and wish them to be. There are a multitude of heavens, each with their own individual characteristics.

In essence, the heaven we go to is a place that is exactly what we deserve, because our minds have created its existence through our deeds and efforts while on the physical plane. Now, don't be quick to call such a belief pure heresy. Before you do, remember that, after His resurrection, Jesus said that He was going to heaven in order to prepare a place for us and that in His Father's house there were "many mansions."

Jesus never said that there was only one heaven. He, in fact, indicated that there were at least several dwelling places where we would go to join the Almighty. For those needing additional quotes from the Scriptures to justify the thinking of the authors, in the Old Testament Moses told of seeing "The heaven of heavens" (Deut. 10:14) and the writer of Kings 8:27 declared, "Behold! The heaven and heaven of heavens cannot contain thee." The Apostle Paul referred to an experience he had while in the "third heaven" where he "heard unspeakable words" (see Cor. 12:2). David, King of Israel, cried out in great ecstasy of spirit, "Praise Him ye heaven of heavens." In Psalm 48:6, he also declared: "By the word of the Lord the heavens were made."

From those who have passed over and returned it has become evident that as a well-meaning person you will find heaven to be a beautiful place where goodness and peace abide always. The material world has its solid walls, streets, trees, etc. and is solid because your mind/spirit has solidified this cosmic hologram due to the fact that the mind must solidify its reality in order to find direction and meaning. Therefore, the dimension of heaven where you will go will be a solid place as well, with walls, streets, trees and so forth.

Heaven is literally a higher level of consciousness; a complete and real new dimension for your consciousness to dwell upon. In order that your soul can reach new heights of awareness, it is very important that you will find your solid and real heaven in exactly the place and within the specific boundaries which you know it to exist. Whatever level of awareness you have progressed to, this is exactly the zone your soul will inhabit in the afterworld. Briefly, heaven is exactly what you think it is! It will be real and solid for you, in exactly the dimension your spirit perceives and deserves.

IS HEAVEN A MILLION MILES AWAY?

How far away is heaven? Will we have to journey for days in order to reach the Promised Land? Hardly, for in the twinkling of an eye following your departure from this reality you will find yourself in another dimension surrounded by those loved ones you long to see again, as well as by those who might be called "teachers." These instructors are there to assist you in your transformation and in general to show you around your new home and tell you what to expect.

Recently, we have seen several articles written by clergymen and by scientists conjecturing that heaven may exist on the other side of a black hole in space or in some other solar system light years away. Such forms of thinking can only originate from those men and women who place reality solely on a physical basis. To their limited minds, heaven must be some place solid. It cannot simply exist here and now, in the etheric. They want to be able to touch heaven, and if they can't touch it then, in order for heaven to be real at all, it has to be far enough away to be out of immediate range of their scrutiny.

Don't be fooled for a minute. Heaven is right above our heads. It is not someplace else. If anything, the truth is that other planets have their own spiritual zones that are populated by a multitude of highly evolved beings even if we can't see them through the telescope. We know they exist because the Bible tells of such encounters (Ezekiel saw the wheel way up in the middle of the air), and our own files are filled to the brim with the experiences of those trustworthy souls who have found themselves face-to-face with beautiful beings who had a spiritual quality about them that is indicative of the fact that they are far more advanced than we are here on this material plane of earth.

Bet you didn't know either that Winston Churchill was once heard to say that when he died he was planning to go to a place 5,000 miles up. Interestingly enough, high altitude radar has often picked up blips of unknown origin coming from just such an altitude. Such blips have often registered as being upwards of five miles across, as if they were some form of "sky-island" floating in the upper regions of our atmosphere. Yet, as massive as these blips are, nothing can be seen through a telescope, indicating we are once more dealing with unseen realms or kingdoms.

Here's an even more shocking, and quite titillating, bit of evidence that the spirit world exists nearby. Several times, while in the limbo of space, our astronauts have heard strange voices coming through their earphones speaking in languages they are not familiar with. On the Apollo 12 mission, one of our lunar walkers actually heard the chords of the song "Where Angels Fear to Tread" while he was bouncing about in the free fall gravity of space.

NASA also picked up the emission but they could not trace its origins, and, since they were communicating on a special channel with the astronauts, they felt convinced that the song was not being broadcast by anyone on earth. Where, then, was the tune coming from?

To our minds this seems to be a way of telling us that the angels of the Lord are always close at hand. Many celebrated individuals – be they well-known show business personalities, politicians, public servants and heroes – besides Churchill know the truth about the afterlife but manage to keep what they know to themselves for fear of reprisal from the organized churches and from spiritually dead society as a whole.

They reason that if a person wants to believe there is only one heaven or one hell and that it is a million miles away, that's their business. From what we have come to understand, each planet in this solar system (as well as throughout the vast cosmos) is made up of various spiritual planes, the lower ones purely physical in nature and the people residing there materialistic in overall content.

This is the type of plane we currently reside on. As we leave the physical by way of the soul, we discover that the planes directly above us are much like the earth, while as we journey higher we come closer to God's kingdom, which is of a spiritual and not physical essence. According to researchers, the eleventh plane is the highest and it is there that you become one with the Almighty, casting aside any remnants of your earthly ways, deeds or thoughts.

LOCATION OF THE SUMMER LAND
– OVER THE HIGHEST MOUNTAIN TOP?

One of the greatest spiritual leaders of our time was Martin Luther King, who did more to spread equality through non-violent means than anyone else we can think of. For all intents and purposes, Rev. King must have had a clairvoyant vision when he declared that he had been to the mountaintop and seen the Promised Land. A survey by the authors shows that many of those near death report being taken to the highest mountain from which they can see the earth far below and their next home not so far away.

Take the experience of a young boy, who, on his dying bed, and with his last breath, beheld and briefly described the Summer Land. The little child was dying. His weary limbs were racked with pain no more. The flush was fading from his thin cheeks, and the fever that for many days had been drying up his blood was now cooling rapidly under the touch of the icy hand that was upon him. There were sounds of bitter, but suppressed, grief in the dim chamber, for the dying lad was very dear to many hearts. Those around him knew that he was departing, and the thought was hard to bear; but they tried to command their feelings that they might not disturb the last moment of their darling.

The father and mother, and the elderly physician, stood beside the little boy's bed and watched his heavy breathing. He had been silent for some time and appeared to sleep. They thought it might be thus that he would pass away, but suddenly his mild blue eyes opened wide and clear and a beautiful smile broke over his features. He looked upward and forward at first, and then, turning his eyes upon his mother's face, said, in a sweet voice: "Mother, what is the name of the beautiful country that I saw away beyond the mountains – the high mountains?"

"I see nothing my child," said the mother. "There are no mountains in sight of our home."

"Look there, dear mother," said the child, pointing upward. "Yonder are the mountains. Can you not see them now?" he asked, in tones of the greatest astonishment, as his mother shook her head.

"They are so near me now – so large and high, and behind them the country looks so beautiful, and the people are so happy – there are no sick children there. Papa, can you not see behind the mountains? Tell me the name of that land!"

The parents glanced at each other, and, with united voices, replied: "The land you see is heaven, is it not, my child?"

"Yes, it is heaven. I thought that must be its name. Uh, let me go – but how shall I cross those mountains? Father, will you not carry me? For they call me from the other side, and I must go."

There was not a dry eye in that room, and upon every heart fell a solemn awe, as if the curtain which concealed its mysteries was about to be withdrawn.

"My son," said the father, "will you stay with us a little while longer? You shall cross the mountains soon, but in stronger arms than mine. Wait, stay with your mother a little longer. See how she weeps at the thought of losing you'?"

"Oh, mother, oh, father, do not cry, but come with me and cross the mountains – oh, come!" And thus he entreated, with a strength and earnestness which astonished all those present. The room was filled with wondering and awe-stricken friends. At length, the boy turned to his mother with a face beaming with rapturous delight, and, stretching out his little arms to her for one last embrace, he cried, "Goodbye, mother, I am going, but don't you be afraid – the strong man has come to carry me over the mountains!"

This impressive testimony is an example of the frequently demonstrated fact that the spiritual existence is revealed, with all its higher and most beautiful forms of beauty, to the refined and exalted sensibilities of old and young at the solemn moment of death. I suppose the idea of a single, all purpose heaven came about because the clergy found it more difficult to express the afterlife in terms of a variety of places that one can go to when they die.

Purgatory, that sort of in-between ground, was the way the Catholic religion handled the problem, realizing that not everyone is all bad and not everyone is all good. But the idea that saying prayers for the dead will enable them to "move upward" toward heaven is not very likely since the dead are responsible for themselves, and there is nothing we can do to help them in their soul's journey.

The truth is that their loved ones will meet them once they've crossed over and give them advice and assistance so that their spirits may progress. One man of the cloth who could verify all of this is likely watching over our shoulder as we write these words. Bishop E. W. Parker died in India on June 4, 1901. Before he passed on, he had an experience which shook his soul, an experience which confirms our faith that there is more than one heaven to choose from.

The story is told by Bishop Parker's best friend and confidante, Bishop Wayne, and is reprinted as follows from the now-defunct publication, "The Christian Advocate."

"When I last saw the Bishop, toward the end of January, the previous night he had a vision in which the Savior appeared to him and gave him the choice of living and suffering or of going to heaven. In the vision, he was carried into what he called the lowest department of heaven and saw heights and heights of glory above him.

"Then the Savior said to him: 'These are My little ones who have received Me but have not had much teaching. If you will choose to come with Me, I will appoint you to teach these little ones.' As the Bishop told me of this vision he said, 'I have an entirely new idea of heaven. I have a new appointment. I am appointed to continue in service for India and teach Christ's little ones. I am so happy, oh, so happy!'"

THE HIGHEST REGIONS

Gabriel Green

Via out-of-the-body travel, many people have traveled to the spiritual realms with no problem whatsoever. Even one of the authors, Tim Beckley, has undergone a soul journey, thanks to the counseling and assistance of Gabriel Green, a Yucca Valley, California, New Age worker. Gabe, as his friends call him, has been in the metaphysical field for over three decades. Back in 1964, he even ran for president of the United States as the "space people's candidate." Gabe collected over one hundred thousand votes, and many of his platform positions, which seemed farfetched then, have since been adopted, such as the admission of mainland China into the United Nations. He was also the first to call for global disarmament, realizing fully well that the world was becoming an unsafe place to live in, largely due to all the nuclear weapons being placed into arsenals by so many countries.

Through a consciousness-raising technique he's developed, Gabe is able to guide those who have a knack for it to higher realms of spiritual existence. The following is a transcription of the session Timothy Green Beckley had with Gabe Green on Nov. 2, 1982, showing what it's like in the regions a few rungs above the earth plane:

G.G.-From your position out of the body, I want you to go to the fourth plane of consciousness. Stand before your fourth plane consciousness and tell me whether it is male or female.

T.G.B.-I'm stuck in a cloud.

G.G.-O.K. what do you see there?

T.G.B.-How do I get out of the cloud? I see a city there. It looks like the city from "Close Encounters." I mean, it's just like a big city in space. I guess I'm there looking at it.

G.G.-Is this actually a spaceship or a city in another dimension?

T.G.B.-I think it's in another dimension. It's there. It doesn't matter whether it's in this dimension or another dimension. It's there right in front of me.

G.G.-What I mean is, if it's sitting on a cloud or if it is a city or is it a mothership?

T.G.B.-I know what you mean. Let me see . . . Yes, it's a city. It's a city in the clouds. I don't know if it's an apparatus or a city. It looks like a city to me. There are people walking around and there are plants growing there. It doesn't seem to be like the Enterprise or something like that. It's a city like the Summer Land or something like that.

G.G.-There are these islands floating in space. It's like they are sitting on a cloud.

T.G.B.-Now, this isn't out in outer space. It's like in a cloud here in the atmosphere. But yet I guess it must be invisible to those here on the ground because I don't know of anyone who's seen it. Yes, it's another dimension. Maybe it's what they call heaven. I don't see any archangels with wings playing harps or anything like that.

G.G.-Well, if it's a little higher than here, it would seem relatively heavenly, relative to earth.

T.G.B.-There's a lot of green. I sense a lot of plant life. There are people going about their business like they have work to do. It's not people sitting and meditating like you might expect in heaven.

G.G.-Is there something that you are supposed to look at there or are just passing through?

T.G.B.-I do see something. There is a person there or a deity or an entity. He's beckoning me. I see him surrounded by a tremendous glow or radiance. He says that he is sending me to earth because I have a mission to fulfill. And I'm happy to do whatever I can to help. He says that it's not going to be easy and I don't have to do it if I don't want to. I say no, I want to go. I want to try to help the people if I can. Apparently, that's what I'm doing now in my own small way. I don't think I was meant to be the president or anything like that. I think I was sent in as a helper. There was a lot that was explained to me then. I see that there are the masters who are helping out with the transition that is going on. Some of these beings you may think of as spirits, but they seem to be working together, the angels, the masters and the spirits. They may be working on different levels of consciousness but they seem to have the same program of operation for the planet. They ask permission to send people here. They tell you what you are getting into before you come down, and you get a chance to select the type of environment that you want to reincarnate into. I guess I always want to take the easy way. I don't want to get in too deep over my head and I have got to the point where they allow that.

G.G.-Some choice in the selection of your parents?

T.G.B.-Not as far as individuals go, but only as to the general type of lifestyle; whether you want to be born into a wealthy family, a middle class family or a poor family. I guess you get Brownie points for the more difficult task. If I had been born into a poor family in some minority group, my consciousness would have been more elevated the next time around. But, I kind of cop out and take the middle road, nothing too difficult, nothing too easy, with a little bit of excitement along the way. They did tell me then that there was a good chance that this would be the last incarnation, that some of us would permanently be taken off the physical plane. They wanted me to try to explain this to people. It is something which some people have to learn and some people will never learn, which is that there is more than meets the eye. There is more than Gabe Green's house here and the rocks outside and the sky and we ought to let people hear about it. Some people know about it and some people don't. Some people have a rough time and some people don't. If Tim Beckley can pull a few people up by the bootstraps and climb the ladder himself and live a fairly decent life, without hurting anyone along the way, all the better. We are all supposed to help each other along the way. The message that man has yet to learn is that we are all brothers and sisters under the skin, and, when you are in spirit, it doesn't matter whether you are rich or poor or black or white or oriental. This is all just a mask that we wear while we're down here. We've got to get over the hurdles and preach brotherhood because that is the cosmic way.

G.G.-Is there something on the eleventh plane of consciousness that would be helpful to look at?

T.G.B.-Am I allowed to look there?

G.G.-Why don't you go up and ask?

T.G.B.-There's a door in my way. It's kind of silly. Should I knock on the door?

G.G.-Yes, sure. Knock on the door. See if anyone will open the door for you.

T.G.B.-I'm trying to knock on the door but my hand goes through it. How do I get around doing that?

G.G.-Ask if it's all right to come in.

T.G.B.-I hear some conversation in the back of the door . . . They say sure, why not, as long as you don't disturb anything.

G.G.-Let's go to the eleventh plane then and stand before your eleventh plane consciousness. Tell whether it is male or female.

T.G.B.-It's not male or female, Gabe. It's a totally different concept.

G.G.-Do you mean it's both, a combination, like an androgynous being?

T.G.B.-I guess that would be the best way to describe it, because it would be a combination of a lot of different elements, the combination of male and female and me and other people as well. It's like a blending of souls. It's like a blending of souls of a lot of people that I love and respect on this plane. I don't quite understand the concept but it is like we were truly one spirit, even though, down here on the physical, we are many different souls.

G.G.-The consciousness is so high on that level that you are all Christed beings; you're sort of one consciousness.

T.G.B.-It's kind of eerie. I sort of have goose bumps thinking about it. I see a giant eye. The eye of humanity is the only way I could think about it. They're telling me to go back, that I will reach this stage someday, but it's not time yet. It's not worth dwelling on what I saw at this point because it's not my stage of development. There aren't that many advanced souls that can relate to that, and it's just confusing. On this eleventh plane, which is the plane of the masters, really, we are all united together as one soul. Ashtar and I are united together on that plane, and he is really me. That's too confusing.

G.G.-No, I understand. If you're all the same consciousness on that level, then, for all practical purposes, everyone is everyone else in terms of awareness.

T.G.B.-At this point I am I and we are we and God is us.

G.G.-O.K. Return to the third plane.

T.G.B.-It's like swish, going down a tube or a shaft of light. No doubt the average reader, with little or no background in such matters, will want to know why such information received through extrasensory means should be considered valid. Isn't it possible that such things are illusions or hallucinations? Of course this possibility always arises, and we ask that caution be our safeguard as with anything we have not experienced ourselves.

"I've worked with several dozen persons to date, helping them to raise their consciousness, and it's always pretty much the same story that comes through them about these higher planes," Gabe explains. "I've guided individuals with no knowledge of such matters and they always talk about the heavenly realms in pretty much the same way regardless of their own religious backgrounds."

This also holds true with what the authors have uncovered in their own spiritual search for deeper knowledge about the higher spiritual planes of consciousness. On the highest level, we are all one soul united, at peace with the universe, and at home with God. What more can we say? But if you feel comfortable with such a revelation, feel free to accept it. Or, if you are so disposed, continue to go on in your own spiritual search.

But remember, there are many facets, many levels to heaven. It is as unique as each spirit is unique. Therefore, you can indeed be assured of going to heaven if your soul reaches out to goodness. The sky, the stars, are truly the limit. Your consciousness is free. God has given it the right to choose its dimensions, its own heaven. You may reach as high as you possibly can. There can be no doubt but that your consciousness (your soul) will continue to progress upward. Not only may you be assured that it will continue, you can know that it will have memory, intelligence and a sense of direction and being.

In short, it will be just as alive and real as it is now in your current physical body. There is only one true death for the soul and that is stagnation. If you do not try to improve yourself as a human being, if you break the golden rule, if you do not attempt to learn cosmic truths and wisdoms, then how can you expect your spirit to flourish? It is not necessary to know all truths . . . only to reach out in an attempt to learn some of them . . . or at least give it a try. In having read this book, you have reached out . . . and will probably continue to do so in many other ways. You are assuring yourself of a "star path" to heaven, a path to a new and higher plane of existence for your soul when this present life is over.

VISITING THE LOWER REGIONS

At this juncture, it is perhaps prudent to consider the likelihood of hell. Does Satan's "pit of darkness" actually exist? And, if so, how do we keep away from its fiery depths? It is our understanding (based upon the first-person testimony of those who have succumbed, if only briefly, to death) that if a person's life has been full of negativity and dread, then, when they cross the road to the other side, they are in all likelihood going to find themselves up against that which they have created in their own mind.

Jesus once said, "So as a man thinks, he does." If a person is full of guilt and his consciousness is not clean, then he will have to suffer the consequences. This is not to say that God is not forgiving, for the Almighty has compassion for all His children, be it a tarnished soul or not. Even the lowest of murderers, rapists, child molesters and cads will get their deserved rewards when it is time to "settle up" with the Lord.

As to whether or not Satan or the devil in a physical form actually exists, we doubt it, though the world – and the universe – does have its "darker" side. Since the creation, the forces of evil – otherwise known as the enemies of light – have tried to take control of this planet and put us through a living hell. They have tortured us both mentally and physically with war, disease, economic instability, starvation and a host of other unnecessary plights which mankind could learn to overcome if he could spiritually rise above it all.

FORTY-EIGHT HOURS IN HELL

George Lennox obviously needed a personal hell in order to rid his soul of the guilt it had obviously collected as a notorious horse thief and murderer of the Old West in the late 19th century. Lennox was serving his second term in prison, and, as part of his punishment, he was put to work in the coal mines during the winter. Quite often he reported that he feared for his safety, but the prison officials ignored his warning and put him back to work far below ground.

The convict, obeying, had not continued his work more than an hour when

103

the roof fell in and buried him alive. He remained in this condition for more than two hours. When he was eventually dug out from under the fallen debris, the doctors were certain that George Lennox's life was extinct. He was taken to the top, and, on examination by the prison physician, was pronounced dead. His remains were carried to the hospital where he was washed and dressed preparatory for interment. His coffin was made and brought into the hospital. The chaplain had arrived to perform the last rites prior to burial. A couple of prisoners were ordered by the steward to lift the corpse from the boards and carry it across the room and place it in the coffin. They obeyed, one at the head and the other at the feet, and were about halfway across the room when the one who was at the head accidentally stumbled over a cuspidor, lost his balance and dropped the corpse.

The head of the man struck the floor, and, to the utter surprise and astonishment of all present, a deep groan was heard. Soon the eyes opened, and other appearances of life were manifested. The physician was immediately sent for, and, by the time he arrived, some thirty minutes later, the "dead" man called for a cup of water and was in the act of drinking it. On examination, he was found to have one of his legs broken in two places and was otherwise bruised. He remained in the hospital some six months and again went to work.

I learned of his experiences while apparently dead soon after from a fellow miner and from his own lips received his wonderful story. He is a young man, probably not over thirty years old. Being a shorthand reporter, I took his story from his dictation. Said he: "I had a feeling all the morning that something terrible was going to happen. I was so uneasy on account of my feelings that I went to my mining boss, Mr. Grason, and told him how I felt and asked him if he would come and examine my coal room where I was digging coal. He came and seemed to make a thorough examination and ordered me back to work, saying there was no danger and that he thought I was becoming cranky.

"I returned to my work and had been digging away for something like an hour, when, all of a sudden, it grew dark. Then it seemed as if a great iron door swung open and I passed through it.

"The thought came to my mind that I was dead and in another world. I could see no one nor hear a sound of any kind. For some cause unknown to myself, I started to move away from the doorway and had traveled some distance when I came to the banks of a broad river. It was not dark, neither was it light.

"I had not remained on the bank of this river very long until I could hear the sound of oars in the water, and soon a person in a boat rowed up to where I was standing. I was speechless. He looked at me for a moment and then said he had come for me and told me to get into the boat and row across to the other side. I obeyed. Not a word was spoken. I longed to ask him who he was and where I was.

My tongue seemed to cling to the roof of my mouth. I could not say a word. Finally, we reached the opposite shore. I got out of the boat, and the boatman vanished out of sight.

"Thus left alone, I knew not what to do. Looking out before me, I saw two roads which led through a dark valley. One of these was a broad road and seemed to be well traveled. The other was a narrow path that led off in another direction. I instinctively followed the well-beaten road. I had not gone far when it seemed to grow darker. Every now and then, however, a light would flash up from the distance, and in this manner I was lighted on my journey.

"Presently I was met by a being that is utterly impossible to describe. I can only give you a faint idea of his dreadful appearance. He resembled a man somewhat but much larger than any human being I ever saw. He must have been at least ten feet high. He had great wings on his back. He was as black as the coal I had been digging and in a perfectly nude condition.

"He had a large spear in his hand, the handle of which was fifteen feet in length. His eyes shone like balls of fire. His teeth, white as pearl, seemed fully an inch long. His nose, if you could call it a nose, was very large, broad and flat. His hair was very coarse, heavy and long. His voice sounded more like the growls of a lion in a menagerie than anything I can recall.

"It was during one of these flashes of light that I first saw him. I trembled like an aspen leaf at the first sight. He had his spear raised as if to send it flying through me. I suddenly stopped. With that terrible voice I seemed to hear yet, he bade me to follow him – that he had been sent to guide me on my journey. I followed him. What else could I do?

"After we had gone some distance, a huge mountain seemed to raise up before us. The part facing us seemed perpendicular, just as if a mountain had been cut in two and one part of it had been taken away. On this perpendicular wall I could read distinctly these words, 'This is hell.' My guide approached this perpendicular wall and with his spear handle gave three loud raps. A large massive door swung back and we passed in. I was then conducted on through what appeared to be a passage through this mountain.

"For some time we traveled in Egyptian darkness. I could hear the heavy footfalls of my guide and thus could follow him. All along the way, I could hear deep groans as of someone dying. Further on these groans increased, and I could distinctly hear the cry for water! Water! Water! Coming down to another gateway and passing through, I could hear, it seemed, a million voices in the distance, and the cry was for water! Water!

"Presently, another door opened at the knock of my guide, and I found that we had passed through the mountain and now a broad plain lay out before me. Here my guide left me, to direct other lost spirits to the same destination.

"I remained in this open space for a time when a being similar to the first one came to me, but instead of a spear he had a large sword. He came to tell me of my future doom. He spoke with a voice that struck terror to my soul. 'Thou art in hell,' said he. 'For thee, all hope is fled. As thou passed through the mountain on thy journey hither, thou didst hear the groans and shrieks of the lost as they called for water to cool their parched tongues. Along that passage, there is a door that opens into the lake of fire. This is soon to be thy doom. Before thou are conducted to this place of torment, never more to emerge – there is no hope for those who enter there – thou shalt be permitted to remain in this open plain, where it is granted to all the lost to behold what they might have enjoyed instead of what they must suffer.'

"Far above me and in the distance I saw the beautiful city of which we read in the Bible. How wonderfully beautiful were its walls of jasper. Stretching out and away in the distance, I saw vast plains covered with beautiful flowers. I, too, beheld the river of life and the sea of glass. Vast multitudes of angels would pass in and out through the gates of the City, singing, oh, such beautiful songs. Among the number, I saw my dear old mother, who had died a few years ago of a broken heart because of my wickedness. She looked toward me and seemed to beckon me to her, but I could not move.

"There appeared to be a great weight upon me that held me down. Now a gentle breeze wafted the fragrance of those flowers to me, and I could now, more plainly than ever, hear the sweet melody of angel voices, and I said, 'Oh, that I might have been one of them.'

"As I was drinking of this cup of bliss, it was suddenly dashed from my lips. I was brought back from my happy dreamland by an inmate of my dark abode who said to me that it was now time to enter upon my future career. He bade me follow him.

"Retracing my steps, I again entered the dark passageway and followed my guide for a time until we came to a door that opened in the side of the passage, and, going along this, we finally found ourselves passing through another door. And I beheld the lake of fire.

"Just before me I could see, as far as the eye could reach, that literal lake of fire and brimstone. Huge billows of fire would roll over each other, and great waves of fiery flame would dash against each other and leap high in the air like the wave of the sea during a violent storm. On the crest of the waves I could see human beings rise, but soon to be carried down again to the lowest depths of the lake of fire. When borne on the crest of these awful billows, for a time their pitiful cries for water would be heart-rending. This vast region of fire echoed and echoed with the wails of these lost spirits.

"Presently, I turned my eyes to the door through which I had a few moments before entered and I read these awful words: 'This is thy doom; eternity never ends.' Shortly, I began to feel the ground give way beneath my feet and soon found myself sinking down into the lake of fire. An indescribable thirst for water now seized upon me. And, calling for water, my eyes opened in the prison hospital.

"I passed through all this and I am as well satisfied as I am that I am alive that there is a heaven and there is a hell, and a regular old-fashioned hell, the kind the Bible tells about. But there is one thing certain: I am never going to that place anymore.

"As soon as I opened my eyes in the hospital and found that I was alive and on earth once more, I immediately gave my heart to God, and I am going to live and die a Christian. While the terrible sight of hell can never be banished from my memory, neither can the beautiful things of heaven that I saw."

HELL FIRE AND BRIMSTONE

Knock on wood, most of us will not find our souls as laden with sin as did poor George Lennox. While we are likely to go through all sorts of personal torment, chances are we will survive and not have to stoop so low as to murder or rob. But what about those of us – the authors included – who might have committed an occasional sin? Will we have to worry about entertaining the same hellish fate as that no good horse thief whose soul seems to be in such an extraordinary state of turmoil? We have no reason to believe that this is the case, as very few of us manage to be "perfect" throughout our lives. Let's face it, there are just too many "temptations" glaring us in the eye.

And furthermore, except for God, what other person has the right to condemn anyone else for their shortcomings? And just what is sinful and what is not? Certainly, to enjoy oneself in a physical way on this, the physical world, is no crime. We should strive to be happy, to be cheerful and to have a good time. God did not put us here to be miserable or to kneel in prayer twenty four hours a day. He made this world beautiful so we could enjoy its beauty. He made food taste good so we would eat it. He made sex pleasurable so that lovers could experience bliss.

There's absolutely nothing wrong with pleasure. Oppressive religions, political parties and emotionally unbalanced moralists are the ones who have tried to shackle our minds and hearts for centuries. They have led us to believe that our bodies are ugly and dirty and that good sensations of any type are against God.

This line of thinking, regardless of its origin, is utter hogwash, and unless you can get such guilt trips out of your mind, you might knowingly be creating your own hellish environment in the afterlife.

Sex, Drugs and Self-Abuse

During your life, if you have been a very materialistic person who has had problems with sex, drugs, smoking or drinking, it is very likely that your spirit body will not rise beyond the first rung or two of the heavenly ladder. Not that this is a crime like stealing or murder, but chances are you will feel more at home – and you will be able to work your difficulties out in a more relaxed setting – if you are closer to that which you enjoyed while on earth.

Warning: Sometimes, if any of these problems have been excessive, the soul will actually make an attempt to cling to the earth plane and will try and attach itself to a person still living who is possessed by identical desires. Through this means, a backward spirit can maintain ties with his former "addictions."

This is the reason why people are warned not to act carelessly with the occult. Tampering with invisible forces you know nothing about can sometimes turn out to be a frightening experience if one doesn't know how to protect oneself. Mental institutions are filled with people who are not able to shake off entities from the lower spiritual planes. These spirits are trying to make a grab for your body so that they can inhabit it and live vicariously through your vices.

This is the reason that we should know when "enough is enough." Almost anything done short of excess is fine, but the body and mind must never suffer, as such suffering is against God's laws of nature and thus to be considered extreme self-abuse. Once we realize the situation, we will know what to look for both on this side as well as the other side of life's curtain. If we find ourselves "trapped," we must find a way on to the next heavenly plane, for that is the soul's purpose in existing.

LINKING UP THE EVIDENCE

Is there additional proof, besides the stories of death bed patients, to confirm the existence of an afterlife? A visual and audio bridge between heaven and the physical world has been manifesting under the guidance of spiritual entities for the past 100 years. People from all walks of life, some knowingly and others completely unaware of what is taking place through them, have been acting as "agents" to prove the existence of the unseen to a skeptical populace.

The methods used by the "other side" include so called "psychic photography" and drawings, spirit writing and music from other spheres. Our own work with prominent researchers worldwide has partly been done to prove that we are able to communicate with those who have passed on.

One of the ways in which we have attempted to prove the reality of the hereafter is through the use of a simple device – the camera. This method of seeing through the veil to the other side was first discovered in Boston in 1862 by William Mumbler, an engraver and amateur camera enthusiast. While experimenting with this then-unique apparatus, Mumbler was surprised to find when he developed some of his first shots that there were extra faces and forms which appeared on the print. Under close examination, he was even more amazed to discover that some of these "extras" were people that he had known who had passed on.

Other early photographers who found their photographic plates "ruined" with images of people who were not meant to be there included Frederick Hudson and French medium Eugene Buguct. Attempts to prove these photo images the work of hoaxers was difficult. Many of the early researchers were out to prove fraud in any way possible; thus, they conducted experiments with psychic photography under what they thought were the tightest of conditions.

But photography was in its infancy, and, since most researchers were unfamiliar with trick techniques, it is possible that many frauds were perpetrated. In 1971, a freelance photographer was on assignment in Central Park to photograph a group of young actors and actresses who were rehearsing for an upcoming performance. Among those there that day was a girl who had appeared in two of filmmaker Andy Warhol's movies.

The photographer took three rolls of film, developing them all the same evening. She printed only those she felt showed the performers at their best. As she went back over the proof sheets a second time, she was puzzled by a cloudlike vapor over the girl's face which showed up only on one negative. She knew that it could not be a faulty print or an accidental image added in the dark room by herself.

Blowing up the negative, she saw even clearer what had only been barely visible on the smaller print. The girl's face was enveloped partly by a fluffy form which had not been visible to any of the others in the park. The camera had captured something the human eye could not see.

But what? And why? When the photographer showed me what she had picked up on the film, I immediately recalled seeing photos of ectoplasm taken during séances held in darkened rooms with infrared film. In many of the cases, the ectoplasm was emanating from the mouths of mediums and on several occasions supported levitating trumpets.

Barbara had obviously caught this phenomena with her camera, and in daylight at that! As unusual as it might seem, the professional shutterbug has managed to cross over to the spirit planes several times, but let her good friend, the well-known psychic, Shawn Robbins, continue the story.

"I had been booked to appear several weeks later to do psychic readings for a group of businessmen at a Manhattan hotel. Among those who I gave readings to were lawyers, airline pilots, doctors and owners of large corporations. Many of their wives were among those who eagerly waited in line for as much as an hour to talk to me.

"The photographer wanted to accompany us, hoping that she could reproduce the strange spirit effect once again. I explained that such shots were a one in a million chance. But, in spiritual phenomena, there is no such thing as odds – for once again her camera caught what no eye could see.

"On several frames, the faces of those present are distorted and rays of light streak haphazardly across the film. Experts have looked at the pictures and have declared them truly unique. One explanation offered is that she might have jerked her camera causing everything to 'jump.'

However, they also admit that if this were the case everything else in the picture would be blurred – this did not happen!

"Thankful for her uncanny ability to capture true spirit forces on film, I sometime later invited her to attend a séance. We were all seated around in a circle, holding hands and concentrating on making contact with any spirits who might have been in the room. All during the séance, Miss Seiler snapped away, unaware of what her camera lenses were picking up in the almost totally dark surroundings. When she returned to her darkroom to develop the prints, she found this time a series of streaks projecting from the area around my head. Apparently, while in a trance, my body had given off psychic energies which showed up on photographic paper."

The question arises, why is this freelance photographer able to get such remarkable photographs when other photographers fail? There is a strong possibility that she is acting as a focal point herself, creating at least part of the energy necessary to produce these manifestations. Dozens of authentic photographs taken by other photographers do exist, of course.

In her book "Master Guide to Ectoplasm," Harriet Hoswell says that the best psychic photo she has ever seen is owned by a Dr. Pierette Austin. It shows an amputee seated in the front row attending a lecture. The man's leg is missing, but in the second photo of the series the "etheric" outline of the man's leg is clearly visible – but casting no shadow, as does the other leg.

At a séance in Philadelphia, the sitters saw weird light bands flickering throughout the room. When photos were developed, all of which were taken in complete blackness, they showed a semi-round ball of light which had left its mark upon the photographic paper.

Photos taken of a medium from Brooklyn show weird light flashes up and down the right and left hand portion of the photographs. It is almost as if "spirit fireflies" were in the atmosphere. Again nothing was visible to either the photographer, the medium or anyone else.

One photographer I showed these photos to suggested the effect might have been caused by static electricity. A second professional discounted this explanation by saying that static electricity did not produce this type of effect.

"Thoughtography has been produced in abundance by individuals who are usually seated in a chair, after having been told to relax and then given a Polaroid camera. Concentrating on a loved one who has passed on, they hold the camera in their hands, aim it at their forehead and snap the shutter. In hundreds of cases, familiar faces appear on the finished film as if the "dead" had projected them there.

In some instances, scenes of unknown locations have shown up on the developed prints. Under any of these circumstances strange figures, forms, structures and events have shown up – again with no sound scientific explanation. Why is the camera able to capture what the human eye cannot see? According to experts, photographic emulsion is very sensitive and is able to record things in a range far above and below what the eye sees. Also, the silver solution in the developer picks up electrical particles which might have been in the air – and since the psychic forces are partly electrical in nature, it picks them up in all their glory.

In addition, when taking spirit photos, the shutter speed should be very slow. This leaves the lens open long enough to capture any stray elements floating in the atmosphere.

TRANCE DRAWINGS AND SPIRIT ARTWORK

Victorien Sardou was born in Paris in 1831 and died there in 1908. During his life, Sardou was responsible for nursing early French psychism and was an accomplished medium who is said to have been able to move heavy wooden objects across entire rooms. One of his spirit guides is reputed to have been Bernard Palissy, a potter who in the mid-1500s produced decorative pottery. Each morning Palissy is said to have taken control of Victorien Sardou's arm and through him produced a good number of drawings and paintings which later sold as rather expensive collector's items.

Kahil Gibran, author of "The Prophet," was a combination mystical poet, philosopher and artist. He believed that art was the "universal language" and drew on his contact with the collective unconsciousness for inspiration. Many of his paintings are vivid examples of spirit art.

Another Frenchman, by the name of Augustin Lesage (1876-1954), had his life drastically altered when he heard a voice tell him while working as a miner hundreds of feet below the surface that "One day you will be a great painter."

One of his truly great performances was revealed in a piece called "The Egyptian Harvest." In this work, Lesage painted a section which is identical to part of a painting existing on the wall in the Tomb of Mena in one of the Pyramids. There is no way that Augustin Lesage could have seen the inside of this tomb; he must have been helped by someone who had been there and is now residing on a spiritual plane. In Baltimore's Johns Hopkins University stands a mural covering two entire floors. Painted by Robert Hieronimus, it is the symbolic creation of the earth from its beginning on Atlantis to its prophetic interpretation of the future of the planet and the rising of this continent. Scattered throughout are UFOs from other worlds, mystical serpents, Biblical references, etc. Hieronimus is an adept who teaches classes in various occult topics at the Aquarian University, which he hopes will be accredited by the state of Maryland shortly.

Cosette Willoughby is an inspirational artist whose drawings are reminiscent of faces brought over from the other side in spirit photography. She recently discovered this unusual gift.

"I purchased a pack of 3 x 5 file cards and a typewriter eraser, the kind you can sharpen like a pencil. I took one of the cards and covered it with the lead from a soft pencil point. Then I dampened my finger in my mouth and smeared the lead. From nowhere faces began to appear. I then took the eraser and went over the card, bringing out the faces more clearly."

Mrs. Willoughby believes that anyone can produce the same effect by following the method which she used. "Once you start making these pictures, you won't want to stop, for each one is so different, and some of them are really art of the kind produced by the masters."

Cosette mentions that your thoughts and moods have a great influence on what comes out in the cards. Her best results were received in a haunted house. She mentions that she is not so much interested in what appears but rather what is causing her to channel her energies in this direction. Perhaps we can all benefit by learning more about this.

SPIRIT WRITING

More than 14 years before the actual sinking of the Titanic, a writer by the name of Morgan Robertson published a book, the plot of which surrounded the fate of a passenger ship on its maiden voyage overseas. In a dream, Robertson saw flags flying and bands playing at the moment the ship was struck from behind by an iceberg.

"It was certainly the most imposing ship I have ever seen," he stated. Although everyone was happy, he could feel some tragedy in the air. "I knew I should warn someone, but how could I when it was only a dream?"

So he did the next best thing. He made an outline of the dream and in two months finished writing a book that he sold to a Boston publisher. It sold so poorly that the book, published under the title "Futility," was soon forgotten by everyone except its author, who realized 14 years later that he had had more than a dream. His book serves as documented proof that man can see into the future.

Other great works have been produced with guidance from heaven. In the early 1880s, a New York dentist by the name of John Ballou Newbrough began writing, under the direction of invisible "callers," a book of some 926 pages. Called "Oahspe," it contained more than a million words and was written at the rate of 120 words per minute, a miracle in itself on an 1880 Sholes typewriter. Much of the material in this book has recently been "discovered" by scientists and deals with such complex topics as space travel, engineering, etc. No mortal man could have known these things!

Music Composed by Spirits

Relatively untrained in playing music, Mrs. Brown has appeared in front of people like Leonard Bernstein, who could find no indication of fraud. Famous composers guide her hands to play and write in manuscript form music far beyond her own skills. World-famed composer Richard Rodney Bennett claims that her talent is absolutely remarkable. "I've no doubt she's psychic. She's told me things about myself she just couldn't have known about otherwise. I was having trouble with a piece of music and she passed along Debussy's recommendation – which worked. A lot of people can improvise, but you couldn't fake music like this without years of training. I couldn't have faked some of the Beethoven myself."

Franz Liszt was the first artist to come to her and stand by the piano and actually guide her hands over the keys. All the other names mentioned come in the same way and her vivid description of their appearance gives additional credence to her explanation of how this music has arrived.

The authors have given the reader various solid examples of how the spirit world is able to communicate their existence to us. When we have come to accept the reality of these other realms, we will find our world a much better place. Spirits have much to offer us in the way of assistance and ask nothing in return except an open mind and a kind heart. We have nothing to lose and much to gain by our link with the next world.

CAN THE DEAD PICK UP THE TELEPHONE
AND CALL THE LIVING?

The title of this chapter may sound like it's asking an absurd question, but the answer is not as obvious as you might think. Parapsychologists (those scientifically trained individuals who study life after death and the question of the soul's survival) have now documented dozens of cases in which those who should not have been able to have communicated across the borders of life to those who can still answer the phone.

Ida Lupino is one of Hollywood's legends. Her show business career spans several decades. In fact, show business has always been in Ida's blood, as her parents made their careers in the performing arts. Often, as a young girl, Ida was left behind with her grandmother in London while her folks toured on both sides of the Atlantic.

One evening when she was nine, Ida found herself in a fitful sleep. She woke up sometime before midnight thinking about a good friend of the family. She saw that he was seriously ill in her nightmare, so she ran downstairs to tell her grandmother about the content of her dream. Once downstairs, the phone in her grandmother's flat started to ring, and, since her grandma was busy in the kitchen, Ida ran to pick up the receiver.

According to Ida's story, which was related firsthand to journalist Danton Walker, the voice on the other end of the line seemed far away but clear enough for her to tell that it belonged to Uncle Andy, the friend of the family she had just been dreaming about.

"The voice became stronger and I could understand the message, which was repeated monotonously several times: 'I must speak to Stanley. It is terribly important.'" Ida turned the receiver over to her grandmother, who also recognized the voice as that of Andy.

"Whatever is the matter?" she exclaimed upon hearing his obviously troubled speech pattern. "I'll tell my husband you called the minute he walks in."

115

Right in the middle of the conversation the phone line went dead. The switchboard operator at the residence where they lived was rung up and she went so far as to deny that any outside calls had been transferred to their apartment that evening. Upon his arrival home, Stanley was given Uncle Andy's urgent message. Immediately, his face became pale and he fell into the nearest chair. Shaking, he informed those present that it must have been someone else on the phone, because Andrew Meyer, the friend in question, had died three days earlier, upon hanging himself!

As eerie and "out of place" with reality as this account may seem, it is by no means that unusual for the dead to be able to telephone the living. Two well-known parapsychologists have, in fact, documented several dozen cases of this very nature. "Phone Calls from the Dead" (Prentice Hall), by D. Scott Rogo and Raymond Bayless, is an extremely fascinating volume which goes into such cases in extreme detail. In chapter two of their book, the authors tell how they had spoken with a woman, a Hollywood actress, who was involved in such a "phone call" back in Texas when she was eight years of age.

"My mother had a very dear friend whose daughter had gone away to college. The daughter came back home around the first of the year, each year. The third year, while on her way back home, she was killed in an automobile accident.

"A couple of years later, we were over at the home of this friend of my mother's for Thanksgiving, which was one of the holidays for which the daughter used to come home. The telephone rang. I was at the age when the grownups were away in the living room and the kids were always running around. I would answer the phone. I picked it up and heard the long-distance operator say, 'I have a collect call.' She mentioned the name of my mother's friend and she mentioned the name of the daughter. This threw me a little bit, even as a child, and I said, 'Just a minute.' I went and got my mother's friend. She came to the phone. I stood watching her, because I had heard the name and thought that maybe somebody was playing a joke on me or something. She listened to the phone, turned absolutely white and fainted."

When the woman came to, the oldsters in the group huddled around her to find out what had brought on her condition. The woman was nearly speechless. Finally, she said that she had heard the voice of her deceased daughter and that the girl had said "Mommy, it's me. I need twenty dollars to get home." Scott and Bayless explain further that before leaving school the dead teenager always phoned home and asked her mother to send her money as she considered this good luck. Once again, as in many similar episodes, the long distance operator was rung up but no trace of such a call having been placed was ever found. The

116

question arises as to how we might go about explaining such a phenomenon as a person receiving a telephone call from the dearly departed.

Quantum physics tells us that ours is a multi-dimensional universe. An infinite number of dimensions cross through each intersect point which composes this dimension. Therefore, as the soul is freed from the body upon death, it merely tunes into one of these many worlds. The world which it is tuned into is of higher consciousness if the soul in transition is of basic goodness and flexibility. And what ties these multi-dimensions together?

Science tells us that the molecular density of a dimension is tied together by electrical energy charges. These energy charges bind these various dimensions together as well as act as the borderland between them all. On what, we might inquire, is the telephone run? It runs on electrical energy charges as well.

Did you know that when you pick up the phone and dial and somebody answers on the opposite end of the line, they are not really listening to your voice as you have transmitted it? Instead, they are listening to molecules that have been broken up at one end of the line and reassembled at the other end, thanks to the use of a minute electrical charge.

EDISON'S DEAD MAN'S GRAMOPHONE

Sure, you know who Thomas Alva Edison was – what American wouldn't? But you're not likely to know that outside of perfecting the electric light and inventing the gramophone, the most respected genius of the previous century also had his bizarre side. According to recently uncovered personal papers, Thomas Edison held a strong belief in several aspects of the occult. He accepted as fact the theory of reincarnation, befriended a controversial medium whom he had engaged in telepathic experiments with, and took life after death so much for granted that he actually had diagrams drawn up for a machine he said would enable each and every one of us to talk to deceased friends.

Like many inventors, Edison was not overly eager about taking credit for his brainstorms. He felt that much of what he put down on paper for the benefit of mankind originated from a "higher source" and that he was simply a vehicle or "channel" through which this information could flow freely.

It is said that he would hold up for hours in his private laboratory, refusing to see anyone, even if they had an appointment. Edison would sit by his desk, his eyes half closed, busy scribbling all sorts of notes and formulas as if he were in "another world."

Parapsychologists who have had the opportunity to examine his original papers feel strongly that much of his work resembles "automatic writing" believed to be transmitted from the spirit plane. As outlandish as such a theory may seem, there is ample proof that it is based upon the truth. For one thing, Edison greatly admired Helena Petrovna Blavatsky. Best known as Mme. Blavatsky or H.P.B. for short, this rather stocky woman of Russian descent founded Theosophy, of which Edison was a member.

Among the beliefs of this religious/mystical order was that a super "root race" had once lived on the lost continent of Atlantis and that the "Masters of Wisdom" guide and inspire us from another realm. Edison was quick to quote from Mme. Blavatsky's 1200-page opus, "Isis Unveiled," which contains all sorts of strange occult tidbits. This volume was said to be Edison's most prized possession, and he referred to it often for inspiration.

Being a member of the Theosophy movement (which attracted upwards of a half million followers at its peak and is still active today), Edison held a strong belief in reincarnation. He didn't see where it was likely that God would have created a soul only to destroy it after a few brief years on earth. Edison's library was stacked with reference works on the subject of rebirth.

One book in particular, "The Finest Story in the World," by Rudyard Kipling, gave Edison a bigger charge than we might get out of watching Seka or Marilyn Chambers going through their pornographic paces on our home video, for the British author's work dealt with a London bank clerk who is allowed a glimpse of a former life as a Greek galley slave.

Indeed, Edison could be most philosophical when he wanted to be, though there are some who are likely to say that he was crazier than the Mad Hatter when it came to speaking his mind on matters of religion and survival after death.

"The soul of man is composed of swarms of billions of highly charged entities which live in the cells. I believe that when a man dies, this swarm deserts the body and goes into space but keeps on and enters another cycle of life and is immortal."

Edison held this position and was not ashamed to talk to the press about such matters, despite the fact that they were more anxious to know about his latest invention than his way out theories on subjects which might have generally been felt only the insane speculated about. After his own death, this peculiar – and highly enlightening – passage was found in Edison's personal diary.

Perhaps, more than any other statement, this quote best illustrates his fascination with the unknown: "I cannot believe for a moment that life in the first instance originated on this insignificant little ball which we call the earth. The particles which combined to evolve living creatures on this planet of ours probably came from some other body elsewhere in the universe."

If Edison were alive today, he no doubt would accept as real UFOs and would likely have invented a device to communicate with the occupants of these silvery disks so many have seen. In fact, if you read between the lines of his most intimate, personal thoughts, you begin to wonder if Edison didn't consider it within the realm of possibility that we might all be "space travelers" destined to live out our future lives on other worlds in space.

"Take our own bodies," Edison explained. "I believe they are composed of myriads and myriads of infinitesimally small individuals, each in itself a unit of life, and that these units work in squads – or swarms, as I prefer to call them – and that these infinitesimally small units live forever. When we 'die,' these swarms of units, like swarms of bees, so to speak, betake themselves elsewhere and go on functioning in some other form of environment."

In all actuality, no matter how farfetched his thoughts became, Edison always thought it best to speak his mind. History shows (despite the fact that it tries to make light of the fact) that Edison was often a champion of controversial causes, especially where the occult and psychic phenomena were concerned. For instance, during the most successful years of his career, Edison befriended an elderly Jew who many thought rightfully belonged in the pokey.

Born in Posen, Poland, Bert Reese had gained a considerable reputation as a clairvoyant. It was said that he could "read minds," and, when the vibes were right, actually see the future. Reese had had a number of minor brushes with the law. These had come about mainly due to his methods of giving tips on the stock market and trying to get the wealthy to invest in a number of his schemes, which included a supposedly perpetual motion machine.

However, this did not stop Edison from taking the elderly immigrant seriously. Not one to have his feathers ruffled by public sentiment, Edison conducted several successful experiments with Bert Reese. "I asked Reese to arrive at my office at a specific time. I did not tell him beforehand what I was planning to do." Edison went into considerable detail in his diary to describe the nature of his "foolproof" test.

"After he had arrived, I called in a workman whom Reese had never met before. I asked the man to go into a nearby room and to take a piece of paper and upon the paper write the name of his mother, where she was born, as well as the answers to several personal questions.

"The workman followed my instructions to the letter. There could have been no way for Reese to know what the man had written down, but he did! He gave all the correct answers, and, in addition, told me how much money the workman had in his pocket."

119

But, still, Edison wanted to do more to test this man's powers. Leaving his laboratory, he walked to another building and with a pencil wrote: "Is there anything better than hydroxid of nickel for an alkaline battery?"

The moment Edison reentered the room where the clairvoyant was, he got his answer: "No, Mr. Edison, there is nothing better than hydroxid of nickel for an alkaline battery."

Edison was dumbfounded. The electrical wizard and the psychic soon began to spend more time together, developing a rather close – and profound – friendship. Edison seemed very interested in showing off his oddball human discovery. He would frequently hold small gatherings in his laboratory, at which times Reese would be asked to "perform." It is said that many scientists and men of letters attended these meetings which Edison described as "séances."

Usually, these guests would go away scratching their head in wonderment, so amazed were they at what they observed happening. On one occasion, Reese described to Dr. James Hanna Thompson, a well-known alienist, the contents of his roll top desk down to the smallest item in a hidden compartment inside one of the drawers. From several of Dr. Thompson's private papers, he wrote down words which he could not even pronounce, words which had special meaning to the doctor.

Unfortunately, Bert Reese got caught up in criminal proceedings when he began to inform the heads of large corporations where they might find fraudulent entries in their ledgers. The police thought he might somehow be involved and he was brought before a New York judge. Just as it appeared he might have the book thrown at him, the controversial seer told the judge how much money he had in a certain bank as well as the contents of a sealed letter the judge had in his private chambers. The case was quickly dismissed.

Said Edison of mental telepathy, ESP and Bert Reese: "I tried to undertake a series of experiments to attempt to transfer the thought of one person to another by all sorts of means but without results. Also, I tried to solve the phenomenon by the help of an electric apparatus fastened to the head of the operators. Four among us first stayed in different rooms, joined by the electrical system of which I have just spoken.

"Afterwards, we sat in the four corners of the same room, gradually bringing our chairs closer together toward the center of the room until our knees touched, but for all that we obtained no results. But Reese has no need for any apparatus or any special condition in order to function. I do not pretend to be able to explain his faculty. I am convinced that the needs of civilization will produce some great discovery by means of men endowed with this power. The rare seers of this generation will become the multitude of the next generation."

It is probably because of psychic Bert Reese that Thomas Edison tried to invent a device which he was convinced would change the entire world. From the above quoted passages, it's obvious that Edison held to the idea that a machine might be built which could actually replace the medium in the séance room. He told only his closest friends about this project, and best that he should, because even they were stunned to learn that their associate had formulated a plan to build a "dead man's gramophone."

"I've never seen Edison more serious in all the years we've been acquainted," reflected a local politician who knew him quite well. "He was literally obsessed with the belief that a device could be built to talk with those who had already passed on. Edison thought it would be the greatest scientific invention of all time."

During the period of six or seven months that Edison worked fulltime on his dead man's gramophone, he wouldn't let anyone come near his office. Only the cleaning woman was allowed inside, and she later reported that his lab was a mess of wires and dials and panels.

"I proclaim that it is possible to construct an apparatus which will be so delicate that, if there are personalities in another existence or sphere who wish to get in touch with us, this apparatus will give them the opportunity. Why should personalities in another existence spend their time working a triangular piece of wood over a board with lettering on it when something much better can be devised?"

Nobody knows why, but Edison never released his strange communications device. His invention, if it was ever completed, appears to have died with him. There are those, however, who claim that Edison's greatest invention of all time was suppressed, and that he was repeatedly warned that such an invention would cause utter havoc and might bring about society's fall. It was theorized that religious leaders wanted Edison to give up working on this device and put pressure on him not to release his findings to the world.

So far only random scattered notes have been unearthed, and so perhaps Edison took what he knew about the afterlife to the grave with him. And while we remember him best for inventing the modern light bulb and laying the ground work for our most advanced recording devices, Thomas Alva Edison's greatest contribution to mankind may still be forthcoming – a machine which will enable us to talk to the dead!

Electronic Voice Phenomenon

And even though Edison may not quite have mastered the means of inventing an electronic device to talk with the spirit world, others just as wise have followed closely in his footsteps and may have managed to take several giant leaps forward for mankind in the last few decades with a device which most of us take for granted – an ordinary tape recorder. It all started in Germany when a man attempted to play back tapes he had made of rare birds chirping in the woods near his home. Upon playing back the tapes, he was able to make out in the distance voices which he had not heard upon making the tapes. The voices seemed to be human and to be calling his name. Listening more closely, the man was shocked to discover that one of the voices sounded exactly like that of a close friend – a business associate who had died two or three years prior to his historic walk in the woods.

He was stunned (to say the least), but repeated experiments brought identical results. Thus the new science of "electronic voice phenomenon" was born. Today, an estimated two hundred parapsychologists in fifteen countries have had positive results when attempting to record the voices of the dead. Respected author and psychic researcher Harold Sherman has listened to hundreds of spirit voices on tape and is convinced they are legitimate and not hoaxes.

One organization operating out of a small office in Severns Park, Maryland, has a file of over 20,000 tapes of this type. Sarah Wilson Estep, who probes this enigma, says that many of the voices tell of a life everlasting and of peace and tranquility not to be found in our physical dimension. The voices also say that there is much to learn where they are and that the afterlife is a vast place, very pretty and very bright.

THE WORK OF DR. MUELLER AND GEORGE MEEK

What Edison might have failed at, a North Carolina man by the name of George Meek may have finally perfected. Working in conjunction with a psychic inventor named William O'Neil, "Spiricom" has successfully been in operation for several years. Used as an "intercom" between spirit planes, this ham radio-like device was actually developed with the help of scientists who no longer number among the living.

The Metascience Foundation of Franklin, N.C., is the brainchild of electrical wizard George Meek who, because of personal evidence, believed it was possible to communicate on a regular basis with the so-called dead. He was helped along in his work by O'Neil, who professed to be clairvoyant, but once they got started on their project they found out that inventors on the "other side" were willing and actually anxious to lend a hand to perfect such a machine.

After much labor, "Spiricom" has become a reality, thanks mainly to the assistance of a deceased physicist, Dr. George Mueller, who helped to iron out the bugs that at first existed in building such a two-way radio between our world and the next. When Dr. Mueller initially started speaking over "Spiricom," those operating the apparatus had no knowledge of who he was. It was only after they asked him repeated questions that his background began to emerge. They checked existing records in other states and found that a Dr. George Mueller had indeed once lived and had taught at Orange College in Costa Mesa, Calif.

Other claims that Dr. Mueller made from the beyond were all proven to be a hundred percent accurate. When asked to help in perfecting the "Spiricom," he agreed, and little by little the quality of the voice transmission began to improve and the messages themselves became of greater length and of more scientific and philosophical importance.

Indeed, listeners can hear Dr. Mueller's conversations for themselves as some of the most important transmissions have now been made available to the public. Interested parties can contact Metascience directly at Box 747 in Franklin, N.C. 28734.

A PERSONAL PERFORMANCE

With the widespread use of the telephone answering machine, it is possible that many of you reading this book will actually, sometime during your life, record for posterity a message from a friendly spirit. Just recently, shortly before work was completed on this manuscript, one of the authors (Tim Beckley) played a tape of a spirit voice which came through to the living in just such a fashion.

Jimmy (not his real name) had attended a spirit circle for the express purpose of asking questions of a deceased friend who had not long ago made the transition to another reality. His friend came in "loud and clear" for more than ten minutes, rattling off descriptions of the kingdom he now occupied.

Just before "signing off," Jimmy's friend announced, "I will speak to you again soon" in his normal tone of voice. A week or so later, Jimmy returned home from work and proceeded to play back the messages on his telephone answering machine. On the tape was the unmistakable voice of his deceased friend saying, "I promised I would speak to you again soon."

Then came silence. So before you run down to the nearest medium and attend a séance, remember that the means to communicate with the spirit world MAY BE ONLY A TELEPHONE CALL AWAY!

QUESTIONS PERTAINING TO THE SUBJECT
OF THE IMMORTALITY OF THE SOUL

There are literally hundreds – if not thousands—of questions we could ask about the world hereafter. Many wish to know about the location of the world of spirits, the appearance of those who dwell in other dimensions, as well as the customs that prevail in these heavenly societies. We're interested in knowing if we are permitted to eat in the great beyond, will we find our relatives waiting for us, will we have a love life, will we be entertained, or are we destined to float around on a cloud for all eternity playing the harp dressed only in a white gown?

A person could literally spend eternity – at least in our timeframe – theorizing about such matters. And then who knows just how right we might or might not be? Naturally, both Tim and I have pondered these very matters, discussing them endlessly upon getting together for periodic brainstorming sessions.

One of the most frequently asked questions is, "Do souls eat, sleep, make love, or simply lounge around in the great beyond?" The answer cannot be given in absolute words which will be applicable to everyone. If you make love with your eternal bond mate, for example, it is indeed a beautiful, eternal and cosmically rewarding experience. Love exists in heavenly dimensions as it does here. However, in the higher planes, love is more closely associated with a blending of spirits so that two become literally as one.

I doubt very much if you'll find singles bars, and one night stands just do not exist as they would be of benefit to neither party. On the higher planes – as we become attuned with God's true vibrations – love becomes more universal in nature, and we find that our spirits no longer crave the company of another soul to offer comfort and support. Until we have obtained these heights, however, we do strike up lasting relationships with other spirits who are on our same wave length.

As for eating, well, some souls have progressed only to the stage in their earthly life where they need "fancy food" in order to maintain mental and physical balance. Some souls of goodness who are definitely headed for heavenly dimensions still will enjoy the pleasures of eating, though it will be done solely for

125

taste sensations since consuming food is not necessary to stay "alive" in these other realms. Eventually, all of us will progress beyond this point, though it could take us quite some time, depending upon how much we learn after crossing over.

MEETING LOVED ONES

Now comes the matter of meeting up with loved ones, friends and relatives in the afterlife. The truth is – and be prepared for a possible shock – if you disliked your parents while you were on earth and never got along, you will not have to suffer meeting up with them in heaven. If your marriage was a bad one (say your wife tried to poison you), there is no need to suffer and prolong the pain after you've "gone." If a relationship was not generally blissful and you have no desire to confront that individual ever again, your soul will not meet up with theirs.

What would be the purpose? During a lifetime, certain souls form links with other souls. Usually this happens easily and naturally within the family structure; the most obvious example is the mother/child link. Just as the mother and child blend lifeblood during the time that the baby is in the womb, so it is that the life-force, the spirits of both mother and child, blend during a lifetime.

Once in a while the mother-child relationship is not that good and one or both do not wish to be psychically/spiritually linked to the other for lifetime after lifetime. In this case, it is the right of the soul not to blend with the other. Occasionally there is a "karmic debt" which keeps two souls together, lifetime after lifetime, for better or for worse.

This type of life-after-life link can be examined and explained by a gifted psychic if the person involved wants this understanding, which stretches past one lifetime. If a link is not made within the family, often two very good friends, lovers or marriage partners form a spiritual link. In this case, these precious and infinite friends await on the other side.

The bottom line is, if the two soul-forces are tied together, they will find each other again after "death," for they have formed a bond which is larger than both of them and which survives death in the mundane dimension. Theirs is a consciousness which is tuned in to the same "cosmic station," and so they will naturally meet on the other side. It is traditional universal law that the bond-partner who made the transition first guides the newly-transitioned partner through the period of death of the physical body and shines a light into the heaven-world of the beyond.

Seldom is there a problem with, for instance, one's mother being on one level of heaven, guiding one onward during the transition and one's marriage partner, with whom a cosmic bond has been formed, awaiting on another level of heaven.

Usually the person making the transition to the afterworld has formed a more definite link with one level of consciousness or the other. However, if there is conflict, gentle guidance from the Higher Realms will make the decision an apparent and easy one as the transition is made. It truly depends on what level the person making the transition is on; if you would not be comfortable at an extremely high level of consciousness, for instance, you will seek your own level slightly less exalted but still within heaven.

Perhaps your mother had reached an extremely high level of consciousness, whereas you and your marriage/bondmate (soulmate) had reached a level with which you both felt comfortable, which was home. In that case, you will go home. Home is your level of consciousness, your frequency, your vibration. It is the drummer to which your spirit marches. It is where you truly feel at ease. It is your dimension!

MARTIN LUTHER KING SPEAKS

Many important and influential world leaders, scientists, religious figures and the famous in general who have passed on still try to guide our actions in order to make the earth a better reality in which to live.

Churchill, for instance, comes across the dimensional barrier frequently to give us discourses, as do the likes of Washington, Lincoln and Kennedy.

If you're more into a "pop" oriented lifestyle, no need to fret, as Elvis Presley and John Lennon also give forth with pearls of wisdom from their new homes. Since his assassination, black leader Dr. Martin Luther King has spoken through a very unlikely medium. Florence Gunn, at age sixty, was entirely skeptical about psychical matters, not being at all informed on parapsychology or spiritual science. Nevertheless, her life became changed when voices started popping into her head. These voices purported to be from departed souls.

Ms. Gunn began keeping a record of the messages she received. On Good Friday she heard for the first time from Dr. King, who continues to want to see the world we reside on become a better place in which to live. And how does Martin Luther King see heaven?

"I behold the glory of the Lord. I am with Him now. All is well with me but is it well with my people? Who will care for them now? There is much to be done for them. I am happy here because I am useful. Could anyone be useful or happy if just walking golden streets, wearing a white robe and singing all day long? What a useless life that would be! No one, but no one, would enjoy it for more than a little while. We need work into which we can put our spiritual hearts. No, we do not hurry and get out of breath here. Neither do we walk the golden streets or loll around in luxurious idleness. We are orderly, busy, neither hurried nor flurried."

Are spirits then expected to be perfect? According to Dr. King, this concept isn't necessarily true. "We make mistakes here just as we did on earth. Being here does not mean that we suddenly become perfect, but we can see further, deeper than we did on earth."

THE DISEMBODIMENT OF MAN

Neither Tim nor I profess to know all there is to know about the afterlife; such a study would take several decades. But one man, Dr. Paschal Beverly Randolph, M.D., put 50 years of his life into such an avocation. Reading all the available literature (religious, historical and psychic texts), as well as interviewing those who had near-death-experiences or who claimed to have communicated with spirits is how the good doctor formulated his opinions.

Many, many years ago, Dr. Randolph put together a 200,000 word manuscript titled "After Death – The Disembodiment of Man," which was based upon his seasoned research. The topics he covered are vast and utterly boundless – just as the regions of heaven are. In order to whet your appetite for more knowledge on this subject, we have drawn from this very literate work to give the reader a better idea of what it's like in the next world.

We have broken Dr. Randolph's thinking down into various categories to make for easier reading.

SPIRITUAL BEINGS OF OTHER WORLDS – SIZE AND SHAPE

The size of an ethereal person is, but not invariably, such as, were they solid substance, would balance from eighty to one hundred and fifteen pounds; albeit, there are in some of the spiritual zones very tiny people indeed, who, having been occasionally seen by earth-dwellers, have been christened Fairies, Fays, and Banshees.

There are others ten feet and over in height; while on the farther zones there are people wholly and totally dissimilar in all respects from those of this solar system. Here is the law: Large earths produce large creatures; small earths, small; and if our moon's inhabitants ever reach the human plane, they will not exceed the height of thirty inches; while the people of Jupiter, Herschel, and Saturn are a great deal larger and finer than ourselves.

The size of the planet also determines the law of duration. We are old men when Jupiterians are mere boys; and their school children would laugh at the mental imbecility of our profoundest savants. An ethereal man cannot penetrate solid matter while organized. Were he enclosed in an iron coffin, he would pass through its pores as sweat through the cuticle, reform on the outside and consider it a very unpleasant experiment, not to be repeated.

An ethereal man could not be annihilated by any means whatever, even though blown from a thousand cannons. Such a thing would shock a man and incapacitate him from thinking clearly for a time, but that is all.

RETAINING PHYSICAL CHARACTERISTICS

Do we retain our physical characteristics, such as hair, eyes, and so forth, in the other life? To a certain extent, as to general form of features, save that deformities are toned down. Our red and other colored hair here is of a general flaxen hue there; it is long and flowing; we are beardless, except as we choose to assume the contrary appearance. Fat men lose their fatness. Nearly all of us there are of a beautiful olive-pearly tint, with the peach-rose in either cheek; our eyes are both light and dark, but not violently so; the tall man becomes shorter; the stumpy man or dwarf increases in stature; and the lank skeleton attains to beautiful and harmonious proportions.

LANGUAGE, BEAUTY, GROWING UP

In reference to vocal language, it is used. At first we speak in our native tongues; but rapidly learn others, because hearing the sounds that convey a man's meaning, and at the same time both feeling and seeing his thought, we soon acquire what otherwise would necessitate long study. The tendency of all vocal speech there is towards a universal Phonetic system, and in the upper grades such is universally used.

But there also we have two other modes of conveying information: one of which is the reading of thoughts, the other, by conforming our features to the required expression, which is readily understood by the developed initiates.

Dr. Randolph formulated the following idea. First: That children grow up there as here; and second, that females generally, though not universally, appear as matrons of from thirty-five to fifty years. Men generally appear to be from thirty to forty-five; while occasionally one is seen as a patriarch and many as mere lads.

A few of earth's celebrities are famous there; not because they were kings and generals, but by reason of the parts they played in the moral, political and religious worlds. Thus, Buddha, Pythagoras, Luther, Plato and others are the centers of great attention and attraction still.

The standards of beauty vary there, according to the tastes of different constitutions, nations and customs. Purity and intellect generally are the criteria; for, as these are possessed, they are reflected on the countenance.

BOOKS AND KINGS

It is asked if there are books there; and I reply yes; but not such as we have.

129

They are on scrolls, not pages, and are picture-written, not typewritten or morocco-bound. There are libraries to which all who wish have access.

Are there kings and rulers there? Yes. But these, except in the lower regions, are such by natural, spontaneous gravitation and selection. Mistakes are never made, for the reason that the right man glides into the right place by a natural process.

Are nations distinct there? At first, and on the lesser planes, yes; but soon a great inter-commingling takes place, as individuals rise from and gravitate out of conditions tending to isolation and non-progress. Whoever would ascertain the condition of the dead of a million years ago must quit the boundaries of this solar system, for none from it are in that sphere, and search for them among the stellar zones of space, where they exist in myriads.

OCCUPATIONS AND RELATIONSHIPS

The next question on the list concerns our occupations in the worlds of ethereal people. To fully reply to it would require not one, but an entire library of books. (a) We retain and acknowledge no relationship there, save such as we have love and friendship for a basis. My father is not necessarily related to me merely because he was the channel through which I came to earth; nor is my mother any nearer to me simply because she received the monad Me, incarnated it in a flesh-and-blood body; nursed me for seven years, more or less, and called me her son and darling.

Ties, blood, race or family count for little or nothing over there; for it continually happens, as said before, that the veriest stranger is nearer and dearer than husband, wife, parent, sister, child or brother; say, even than those we sometimes believe to be our "Eternal Affinities."

And one of our occupations there is the study of the laws that govern this subject. Kindred there is based on homogeneity, not on consanguinity or external law. We love those who love what we do, and these are our brethren and sisters. Two cannonballs are not necessarily related because cast in the same mold; nor are people brothers or sisters merely because their parents were the same; for their natures may be, and often are, wholly opposite and antagonistic.

Nor is it unusual to see a coarse, rough, brutal, lowly-organized man and a girl born of the same couple who is fine, gentle, sensitive, intellectual and spiritual, to a very high degree. Where's the relationship? In what does it consist? The study, then, of psychical law will afford scope for the best minds in the spiritual worlds.

Names (b) "What's in a name?" someone asks. A great deal, I reply. There are long catalogues of names and what they represent to be learned, and, in one single branch of nomenclature, that of botany, we have abundant occupation in the study. Then there is architecture, history, algebra, the higher mathematics, government, ideology, phonetics, music, melody, harmony, vision, acoustics and ten thousand other arts and sciences to engage our attention and occupy our thoughts.

Speaking of names reminds me that those given us or assumed here go for naught in our upper homes. There are no John Smiths there; nor is Mynheer Johannes Von der Spreuchtlinsaber any longer compelled to respond when hailed by that formidable appellation.

We convey information to other souls telepathically for the most part, so they know by our vibrations when we are directing our thoughts to them.

Old names, then, are dropped soon after our arrival there – albeit, if an earthly sufferer yearns for the ministrations of an ethereal friend whose name might once have been John Truman, or William Hardy, his electric summons will reach him in the upper land, wherever he may be.

Every person's quality is expressed upon the features, just as the unspoken thought is mirrored on the tablet of consciousness. Like that, too, it can be read, unless, indeed, as is possible in both cases, but only by a painful, continued effort, the person wills to conceal the thought or give a false impression to the features, and that general quality or a peculiar trait determines the name by which the person will be known.

Now, the combination of qualities and traits are simply infinite, and so are the names of the myriads who possess them. No two are alike. No language could express this multitude of qualities and specialties. That can only be achieved through and by the celestial phonetics of the spheres.

For instance, Olive Selk, of Janesville, Honey Lake Valley, California, was the peerless and redeeming spirit of that town, a gentle, tender, affectionate and loving soul, qualities expressed in the higher phonetics by the sounds ZOI-LI-VI-IA; hence her most beautiful name will be ZOLIVIA.

Mary Winthrop may on earth possess qualities, social and intellectual, which not only stamped her as a genius but also made her the cherished idol of society. She will therefore be known as EU-LAM-PI-IA, Eulampia, Greek, Evlambea, Anglice, Bright-Shining Light.

THE SENSES

Roses emit sweet odors, yet not all the fragrance of the Gulistan, ten thousand times refined, can equal the blessed aromas that float upon the breezes of the happy land of educated souls!

COLOR

Prismatic hues are fine; the flash of sparkling diamonds transcendently beautiful, while the play of colors in polarized light is vastly more splendid still; but no man of earth, save through clairvoyant intromission – and that is extremely rare – ever yet saw, or even imagined, the superlatively magnificent melody of hues and tints or the ineffable brilliance and glorious beauty of the flowers blooming there!

MUSIC

Ah, how shall cold human language convey an idea or sense of the transcendent melodies, tones and exquisite sounds heard and felt in the upper divisions of the spirits' home, whereof I am writing? It is impossible! I dare not undertake the hopeless task; and yet it will, one day, be described. Those who have listened to Offenbach's opera, "La Duchess de Gerolstein," will remember the exquisite orchestral overture to the third act just before Fritz's disaster. Well, I am positively certain that that piece of music came to him complete, and note by note, from the Spirit Land!

SCENERY

Imagine your highest ideal spread out before you; deck it with the most regal and imperial cities, every house of which shall be a perfect palace; surround it with parks, adorned with trees, whose fruit and foliage shall be unequalled save in a poet's or a lover's dream; let there roam beneath these trees, or stand under their outspread branches, parties and groups of loving men and women, all of whose forms are fair and faultless; females of transcendent grace and beauty; men looking every inch as kings, of intellect, and royal, gentle manhood; children lovely as the summer sunshine, gay as mountain-birds; animals, compared to whose forms that of the gazelle is dull, lame, and crooked; and when you have all this in your mind's eye, believe me when I say, it is no more equal to the reality up there than a cedar swamp is to a king's garden!

TASTE

Flavors! Wait till the nectar is quaffed and the ambrosia tasted by yourself, for no human tongue can tell, no pen explain them, or even intimate their scale or gamut.

TOUCH

Contact! Ah, my God! I have attempted, and may again, attempt to describe them; but as I look at my descriptions, glowing and impassioned though they be,

I am sensible of having failed to convey even a dim and faint notion of the thrilling raptures and exquisite joys of touch and contact awaiting us all over there and now being experienced by countless billions who have gone before!

PEACE, FEASTS AND PLENTY

Buddha's Loaks, the Moslem's Paradise, and the Christian's Heaven are conceptions cold and tame compared with the realities of man's home in the higher divisions. There blessed peace reigns supreme; harmonious melody prevails; God, not man, or creeds, or a book, is there devoutly worshiped; love underlies, will compels and lofty wisdom directs all movement there. Rest and labor alternate, God rules through magic-working law, to which all most joyfully assent; order prevails on every hand and chaos is unknown!

Feasts, parties, balls, operas, concerts, the drama, straws, schools, colleges, universities, libraries, museums, lectures, theatres, orations, celebrations, congresses, elections, coronations – in fact everything good that man here enjoys he also has there, in the upper country, with the exception of genuine law courts, churches, baptisms, and funerals; and some of the glorious scenes there exhibited immeasurably surpass the most ecstatic vision of poet, voluptuary, enthusiast or dreamer.

EDUCATION

The scope, sweep, and extent of the entire human being must ever enlarge: mental, like physical motion, gives heat, and heat expands its subject and object. As we advance in the spirit, as in this life, new, higher and better and nobler ideals are conceived, and we are impelled by the law within to work up to, and act on, those ideals, whatever they may be; and whether they interest the personal, social, moral, aesthetic, religious or intellectual departments of our nature.

New possibilities will ever be attempted and achieved, albeit nothing whatever can permanently endure until the pressure will expand them and thus make room for more ere tomorrow shall end. True, the soul may rest satisfied for a while, and a long while; but the monotony will at last be broken, and it will sight and seek for change. Action is the law of true life, multiplied and varied action. Eternal sameness means eternal stagnation.

NEVER ALONE

The love of thirty years is not the love of eighteen or forty-five. No one goes alone from earth to Spirit Land. Some loving one is always by his side or hers, from the last breath till eternity grows bald and grey. No one goes alone from one grand division to another; no one can gravitate from a low to a higher state before he or she is fully fit to do so and then they graduate in couples.

But it does not follow that those loving classmates or kindly ones are ever the same persons. It were a poor heaven if only one true soul sincerely loved us. If comrade A, in division three, is not prepared to go with B to division four, then A's place is immediately taken by C or D, who are prepared, and the union thus based on fitness for far closer than that just dissolved.

NO TWO SOULS ALIKE

"As like as two peas!" Well, no two peas are alike, nor any two persons in existence; no two souls can develop alike, in all respects and at the same rate, because no two can be exactly similar; and if they were, the chances are a million to one that this one forges a little ahead of the other, or that one springs a mine without the other's sphere. The chances are infinitely against their remaining alike for any given period.

Their earthly experiences could not have been parallel, and a single reminiscence, a memory, may beget a change that will establish a divergence of eternal duration. A tone heard, a flash of light, motion seen or felt by one of the parties, may beget a movement that in time would completely change the entire mental and emotional constitution, just as continued grains of poison would modify the body that took them.

For this reason, then, that no two souls can forever develop in parallel lines, one of them must, in time, diverge from, advance beyond, rise above, or constitutionally change, outgrow or off grow the other; the "eternal" affinity must be considerably foreshortened and lopped off here and there, until common sense makes all clear, plain, right, and the Infinite wisdom be vindicated.

Yet souls are made in pairs; but this involves perpetual friendship, but by no means eternal marriage; it requires opposites for that; but our twin is very like ourselves.

EDUCATION

In this fifth division, there are many colleges and universities in which spirit, its laws, static and dynamic are taught. Memory, the laws of thought; the statics of life; the principles of social evolution; light, its sources and nature; esoteric laws of life; embryology; the integral and differential calculus, direct and in their application to various branches of human learning; philosophy, astronomy, paralactic calculations; the higher mathematics, algebra, and the true theory of the higher equations, psychological law, and a hundred sciences not yet evolved by, or sent down to, man on earth; the laws and dynamics of beauty, harmony, melody, form, government, religion, God, the laws governing friendship, affection, love, the source of the generation and growth of thought, and a thousand things beside.

The people are extremely refined and seem to have decreased in size from what they were in the grade below. They partake of fruits and various aromas, bathe for pleasure's sake and certain ends to be obtained and already explained.

They are mainly sustained by what they absorb and inhale. They sleep, as do all others, and are refreshed thereby. There are no crowded cities; nor is the scene entirely rural; but their houses, cots and palaces are scattered at convenient distances apart over a vast area of surface. They frequently visit the divisions above and below them and occasionally they visit other realms of human abode, just as we here are intromitted to higher ranges of being occasionally.

ETERNAL YOUTH

Reader, come with me and share this vision; gaze upon these glories – all to be yours and mine – one of these approaching years. Look down yonder sylvan glade and behold these hundreds upon hundreds of sylph-like human beings of either sex. They are not of our times or our form of mind; they are Phoenicians, Babylonians, Ninevites, Arabs, Persians, Egyptians, Hindus, Moors, Chinese, and some from Central Africa, some from Greece, and some from old Etruria and the site of storied Troy.

Many of them immigrated from earth ten thousand years ago; some longer than that; and very few of them less than half that vast period over five and thirty years of age! They have drunk at the fountain of perpetual youth and partaken of the fruit of the life-conferring tree.

The females! How like peerless queens of Grace and Beauty! What holy love and tenderness beam from every eye! What melting passion dwells on every lip! How like clouds of lovely glory they move along; and what amazing perfection sits crowned on every feature!

And all of them were once poor, weak mortals like you and I; vexed at a trifle, pleased at a straw; small in spirit, cramped in mind and warped in soul, heedless of all but what the fleeting hour afforded of pain, mixed joy!

But, regardless of what Dr. Randolph's thinking may be, we must always remember that the only instrument we have to perceive our reality (our dimension) at this very moment is our mind/soul. It is exactly the same in the heavenly dimensions! God and the heavenly hosts always "stand at the door and knock."

They are one with us through our intuitive gifts (truly divine conduits to God) and through the goodness of our heart and soul. It is the easiest thing in the world to be in contact with God and with the heavenly hosts. What is not so easy is to know absolutely, beyond a shadow of a doubt, that God lives within us, within our souls, as well as on the outside, in the universe.

Your soul is the God-spark! It is assured a place in the heavenly dimension of its choice if only it knows this, instinctively and intuitively. This is true awareness . . . the awareness of one's rightful place within the cosmic scheme of it all. You are important even though you are a mere particular in the vastness of God's universe. You are made of "cosmic stuff," you are made of "holy stuff." The very life-force which gives you energy to take a breath and to keep your body's heart beating proves beyond a shadow of a doubt that you are "magical" (your soul is "magical"!)

You are eternal, for you are mind-energy, and mind-energy cannot be destroyed. God gave you this mind-energy which is so magical and so mystical. God gave you a particle of Himself/Herself when He gave you LIFE. Rest assured that this life-spark will move onward to its rightful heavenly home!

UFOS – HOW DO THEY TIE IN WITH THE DEAD?

As veteran researchers of the UFO phenomenon, we have come across some very bizarre stories in our line of work. And while the public may have no way of being aware of the actual intricacies of this worldwide enigma, those who have plotted and probed the appearance of so-called flying saucers can tell you that not all UFOs are nuts-and-bolts hardware from space but some seem to be a type of ethereal apparition.

Rev. Billy Graham has suggested in his writings that a percentage of UFOs might actually be angels. After all, religious texts often describe how these heavenly beings arrive in a brilliance that is so stunning to the eye as to make a person go momentarily blind. Also, in the majority of cases, the crews of these glittering vessels appear to be humanoid in appearance, though perhaps just a bit too beautiful to be earthly in origin.

Biblical students will confirm that the angels of the Old Testament were said to be so exactly like us that they would often come into a person's house and eat a meal with them. The only way that someone could tell they were not "ordinary" was by the fact that they sometimes had a strange halo or glow about them, and besides they are always said to be extremely beautiful. A mere coincidence? We'll let you decide.

Now, here's an absolutely fascinating episode that came to our attention five or six years ago. A woman was driving along an isolated stretch of road in Indiana when she saw this circular-shaped device come down and block the path of her automobile so that she could not continue on her way home. Though she was frightened, the woman could not move. It was as if she was paralyzed. Shortly, a hatchway on the side of the craft opened and two beings came out and began walking directly toward where she was seated, frozen behind the steering wheel of her car.

"One of the men stood in the shadows and I could not see him plainly at first," Norma told her tale, a trace of bewilderment obvious in the tone of her voice. "This one fellow, however, came to within a foot or so of my half-opened window.

137

He did not speak, but still I could hear him talking to me, if that makes any sense. He said that he meant me no harm and he wanted to know if my name was Norma. Well, to say the least, I was totally shocked that this complete stranger – and I mean that in its truest sense – would know who I was, especially since I was certain he wasn't even from the same world I lived on. Somehow, I managed to choke out an answer and to inquire as to what he wanted with me. In my mind flashed the following words, 'We've come to show you that you are immortal and that life goes on even after death.'"

At that moment, the second figure who had been off to the side stepped out of the darkness and Norma found herself in total shock. "The man who approached me was dressed in coveralls of some type, and his head was slightly elongated, though otherwise he could easily pass as one of us. But the second fellow, well, I'd know him anywhere. He was dressed in an ordinary shirt and a pair of jeans. The second figure was that of my deceased husband who had been killed in a hunting accident about seven or eight months back."

Norma couldn't control herself. "I began to weep uncontrollably, and, with my tears, came the thought, 'Fear not my darling, as I am with you always in the clouds!' The voice was unmistakably that of my beloved husband, who as far as I was concerned had passed away almost a year ago."

Was there a possibility that she might have been in error, that her encounter with a UFO might have caused her severe mental trauma and that she was imagining at least this part of the experience?

"Absolutely not!" Norma insists. "I'd know my George anywhere." And how did he look? "Better than he had at the prime of his life," comes the widow's response. "He looked slightly ill and pale toward the end, but now he was standing straight, had lost ten or fifteen pounds and the color had come back to his face."

With this, the beings reentered the device that still rested on the roadway, and within seconds it had vanished, traveling at incredible speed straight up into the star filled heavens.

THE CASE FOR GEORGE ADAMSKI'S RETURN

A peculiar story we'd agree, but this incident does not by any means stand alone in the history of UFOlogy. Take the case investigated by British flying saucer investigator Jimmy Goddard, who attended a lecture on June 7, 1965, and found himself in the middle of a most bizarre tale.

"A most unusual incident began on June 7th at about 10:30 p.m. and the witness, an M. Bryant, was just going to bed at his home in Scorriton (England) when he heard a sound like that of a ship's turbine. He looked outside and saw a

Incredible as it may seem, among those who may have returned to an earthly state of presence is contactee George Adamski (as Yamksi) and labor union boss Jimmy Hoffa.

pale blue light traveling west to east at an altitude of 300 to 400 feet. He saw this come down, then the light and the noise disappeared.

"Next day he looked over the area and found strange pieces of metal, some like turbines with curved blades, and some looking like more complicated pieces of machinery. Also there was a glass phial with some silver sand in it (later analyzed and found with certainty to be silver sand). Also in the phial was a message 'adelphos adelpho' (brother to brother) in what appeared to be classical Greek. There was also an evil-smelling patch of jelly-like substance where the object had appeared to land but this quickly evaporated.

"Late that same year (1965), Mr. Oliver, in his capacity as membership secretary of BUFORA, sent a questionnaire round to as many interested people as possible. And one of the questions was: 'Have you ever had a sighting or contact?'"

One of these forms was sent to Mr. Bryant describing an extraordinary contact in which the witness claimed, on April 24th, 1965, to have met with beings from outer space, spoken with them and entered their saucer.

"On the day in question he was going for a walk from his home to Scorriton Down, and when he arrived there he turned to look back toward the village. He saw a large saucer appear out of thin air over the field, then descend to about three feet altitude and hover there. An opening appeared in the middle of the saucer, and a door appeared to slide upward. Three beings, all dressed in 'diving gear' (complete with helmets) came out, and one of them beckoned wildly to Mr. Bryant."

Goddard continues in his communication to this writer by saying that Bryant went over to them, and as he did so they took off their helmets.

"Two of them were definitely not of this world. They had very long foreheads, blue eyes (which reminded Mr. Bryant of cats' eyes), blond hair and squat noses. Their mouths appeared bluish, but Mr. Oliver said that this could be a reaction to our atmosphere. The suits were one-piece and silvery in color, and when the beings moved the sound suggested tinfoil. They had belts with a strange 'sun' or 'flower petal' symbol on them. The helmets had windows in them which appeared to be of a perspex-like substance, and at a place corresponding with the ears there were strange coils.

"The third occupant was different from the other two, although dressed in a similar suit. He had the appearance of a 14 year old boy with black hair, and the suit appeared to be too big for him. He had what Mr. Bryant described as a 'mid-European accent with a touch of American.'"

Goddard then says that this third being talked to Mr. Bryant and this is the gist of what he said: "One month from today, we will bring proof of Mantell. Watch for the blue light in the evening. Danger of forces from Epsilon, who take people for procreation purposes. These cause what you call poltergeists, which are only invisible because of your ignorance of the orbital plane. My name is Yamski."

When asked where he was from he said, "From Venus. If only Des or Les were here, he would understand."

Mr. Bryant then asked if he could arrange for "Des or Les" to see him, and Yamski replied, "No, we will arrange for them to see you."

Goddard continues with his communication by stating that, after this, "Mr. Bryant was helped up into the ship (still hovering at about 3 feet) and found inside that it was made of several identical compartments. In each one there was a door leading in the floor like the one through which he had entered. There was a couch in each compartment, fitted with straps, and a large screen similar to a TV screen on which rainbow-colored lights appeared to be moving upward.

"Mr. Bryant asked how the craft was propelled, and he was told, 'Ideo motor movement.'

"Shortly after this, he was taken out of the craft, which then ascended to about 40 feet, then vanished in the same manner in which it had arrived."

Unless you have a background in UFO research, or have read a ton of books on the subject, chances are you will immediately want to dismiss the entire episode as hogwash before even making a stab at going any further. But just let us get a word in edgewise and say that in the last six – close to seven – decades since UFOs have become a worldwide phenomenon, over two thousand individuals spread across the planet have reportedly come in contact with some type of alien being. Often these stories seem totally off the wall and one's first honest reaction would be to say that the witness was a bit daffy, but, incredibly enough, often those involved are highly thought of, very sincere individuals who seem to have no motive for lying nor have they had a history of mental disorder or hallucinating.

Something strange is definitely going on in the heavens directly above us, but the question remains, what does all this mean? Mr. Oliver, Britain's top authority on UFOs, we're convinced had no prior knowledge about interplanetary craft, but yet he appeared to be telling his experience in all earnestness and as if it had actually happened.

Even more remarkable was the fact that Mr. Oliver had absolutely no way of knowing that an individual by the name of George Adamski (sounding nearly the same as Yamski) had died a scant two days earlier in a Washington, D.C., hospital. Adamski, for those who are not familiar with this name, was one of the earliest of UFO contactees. As far back as October, 1946, this mild mannered man of Polish descent had been among thousands of San Diego residents who were startled to see a gigantic spaceship hovering over a nearby mountain range.

The craft returned over a period of several years, and it was from these observations that Adamski was made curious about who piloted these silvery craft and was confident that he could make contact with their occupants. In November, 1952, Adamski heard that some of these ships had actually been seen coming down in the California desert. So, on November 20, 1952, Adamski invited a group of friends to accompany him to the desert for a picnic and to look for saucers.

Parking off the main highway, it was only a half hour before their "saucer-watch" drew positive results. Attracted first by the sounds of a plane's motors, they "suddenly and simultaneously" saw close to the nearest mountain range a "gigantic, cigar-shaped, silvery craft without wings or appendages of any kind."

The craft seemed to drift in their direction, then stopped and hovered motionless. Adamski excitedly told those with him to remain where they were while he approached the object at a closer range. Setting up his camera equipment, Adamski saw a scout ship maneuver between nearby mountain peaks. The craft proceeded to land and a being got out. He was about 5 feet 6 inches in height and looked to be about 150 pounds. Adamski described him as having "an extremely high forehead; large, but calm, gray-green eyes, slightly aslant at the outer corners; with slightly higher cheek bones than an Occidental, but not as high as an Indian or an Oriental; a finely chiseled nose, not conspicuously large; and an average size mouth with beautiful white teeth."

Through the use of sign language and telepathy, Adamski was able to find out that this being came from the planet Venus. Although he had landed in the desert in a small scout ship, he indicated that all travel outside the atmosphere of Earth was done in a larger carrier or "mother ship." After a few more minutes, and a few more questions on Adamski's part, the space visitor climbed back into his parked ship and took off.

Adamski then returned to the waiting party who later signed affidavits to the effect that such an encounter had actually transpired. The rest of Adamski's story is history. Before passing from this dimension, he wrote several books detailing his encounters with fair-haired space beings *("Flying Saucers Have Landed," "Inside the Space Ships" and "Flying Saucers Farewell").*

His first effort was co-authored by a British historian whose name was – are you ready? – DESMOND LESLIE. Yamski had proclaimed during his meeting with

Mr. Bryant that if only "Des" or "Les" were present, that he would know what was going on. Coincidence? Imagination? A visual hallucination? A pack of damn lies?

All the above could be the explanation to this case history, but maybe— JUST MAYBE!—Mr. Bryant was on the level. In his favor was the fact that investigators saw no traces of UFO literature in the witness' home, nor did he have a history of being interested in the occult or supernatural. Instead, the interviewers found Mr. Bryant to be about 50 years old, married with three children. He told them further that the saucer had the appearance of platinum, and that the sheep in a nearby field had seemed unconcerned during the time the ship hovered, but when it left they turned their heads as if to follow the flight of the craft, which he could not see.

Yamski also mentioned the name Mantell. Well, Captain Thomas Mantell was the name of a U.S. Air Force pilot who was killed over the state of Kentucky when his fighter plane got too close to a gigantic disc-shaped object and he lost oxygen and plunged to the ground, where he was killed instantly.

FROM INSIDE THE UFO, A SHRILL VOICE SHOUTED -

"I AM JIMMY HOFFA! I AM JIMMY HOFFA!"

Now here is a tale that even I – on my sometimes gullible days – find difficult to believe.

Everyone has a theory as to what happened to labor boss Jimmy Hoffa.

We all know he had underworld connections, and we are not talking about the Shaver Mystery here!

History tells us he went out for lunch and never got to look at the dessert menu.

Some say he is buried at the fifty-yard line at Giants Stadium in Rutherford, New Jersey. Others contend he was thrown to "gators" in the Everglades, while there could be a steel drum with his waterlogged remains at the bottom of one of the Great Lakes.

Your guess would be as good as mine. Even the FBI has to shake their head and wonder what became of the infamous Teamster.

But, now dig it, has anyone ever thought there might be a UFO connection? A connection that could place a possibly deceased individual inside a ship from another world?

If the story had been attributed to anyone else, I would most likely have ignored it, but Jerome Clark never wrote for **"The Weekly World News."** In fact, he is an associate at the Center For UFO Studies, an organization founded by the late astronomer, Dr. J. Allen Hynek, who at one time had ties to the U.S. Air Force's Project Bluebook. Jerry is a no-nonsense type of guy who is not prone to UFO pranks. So, when he tells us the story of Jimmy Hoffa calling out from inside a landed UFO, we had better not dismiss the account out of hand.

The incident in question took place in Pelham, Georgia, on August 6, 1977, as Clark relates it.

"The alleged witness is one Tom Dawson, a 63-year-old retired automobile dealer who lives in a trailer park outside that southwestern Georgia town, population 4,500. Even he admits that he doesn't expect anyone to believe his story; he says he wouldn't believe it either if it hadn't happened to him. That's a remark all too many UFO witnesses have made.

"But Dawson says, 'I don't care what they say. This is the honest truth. I'm not crazy, I wasn't drinking, and I've never had a mental condition. This is the very first time I have ever experienced anything like this.'"

On the morning in question, Jerry Clark tells us, the witness "went for a stroll with his two dogs. He stopped over at a neighbor's house and played for a time with Jimmy and Linda Kolbie's baby, then set off for a fish pond located behind some pine trees. To get there, he had to cross over a pasture where about 40 cows quietly grazed.

"He had just stepped inside the gate when a strange circular object suddenly flashed out of the sky and came down in front of him, hovering two feet off the ground. Dawson found himself paralyzed, unable to move a muscle, and noticed that his dogs and the cattle were similarly 'frozen.'

"As soon as the UFO stopped, a hatch opened and five humanoid beings, three men and two women, stepped out. Their skin was pale white, their noses sharp and turned up, their ears pointed. They had no necks. Two, a male and a female, were completely nude. There was no hair on any of their bodies.

"The first to emerge from the UFO, whom Dawson took to be the leader, stepped gingerly to the ground and then motioned for the others to follow. Two men came out and stood at the entrance to the ship, acting apparently as guards. The others then walked out and cautiously approached Dawson.

"Their clothing was 'beautiful' and the men and women dressed alike (except, presumably, for the two in the buff). They wore shoes made of a silky substance, and the toes were pointed upwards.

"Dawson was given what he took to be a medical examination in the pasture. The beings placed a 'skullcap' over his head; the 'cap' had several cords attached to a ring-like device on which there was a set of dials. The UFOnauts lifted Dawson's shirt and removed his trousers."

At this juncture of the encounter, Dawson heard a high-pitched voice screaming from inside the craft.

"I am Jimmy Hoffa! I am Jimmy Hoffa! I am Jimmy Hoffa! I am . . ." The cry, we are told by Clark, was suddenly stifled as if someone had put his hand over the speaker's mouth.

At this point, Dawson was anxious to get the hell out of there, so he kind of backed away as two of the males started "eyeing him" as if they would welcome him as a guest onboard their vehicle, though Dawson saw no reason to join Jimmy Hoffa – living or dead.

The hatchway eventually closed and the ship ascended to about seventy-five feet before it zipped off, taking the crew and presumably the labor boss with them.

Of course, we can't say for certain what the physical density of the ship, its crew or its well-known passenger might have been. It could well have been a prank or it could be that Jimmy Hoffa was calling out from "the other side." It's frightening to think that he was paying the devil his due and that he was not going to Heaven but might have been on his way to Hell.

Or perhaps I am just being a bit overly dramatic.

You must decide.

THE CASE OF UNCLE ROY

Now let's take a case from Diane Tessman's files and do our best to compare it to the above episode just before we try to make heads or tails out of the situation of how UFOs tie in with the dead. There are several cases I know of where a person has died in the regular world and has then been spotted in a UFO encounter. One in particular has to do with a man we shall call "Uncle Roy," who had pursued his interests in UFOs, metaphysics and heavenly dimensions throughout his life.

Some of his relatives even made fun of this interest. Uncle Roy was not married but his nephew James lived with him on his small farm in Indiana, helping him care for a small herd of cows, some chickens and tending the fields. I interviewed James shortly after Uncle Roy's death and the young man had turned from a pessimist who gently had made fun of Uncle Roy's beliefs to a true believer in the paranormal and UFOs in particular.

He gives the following account: "Uncle Roy always claimed he'd been visited by these UFO beings back in his early manhood when he was out there on the back field, getting it ready for the spring planting. But I never really believed him. Oh, I thought that he thought he was telling the truth but I just sort of figured that Uncle Roy was unique and that sometimes he told tall stories that even he believed."

James shakes his head and lights a cigarette. "That's what I used to believe.

146

Now I betcha I sound just like Uncle Roy to you. I bet you are thinking that I believe this story but that I'm just a crazy farm boy."

I assured James that I myself have had UFO encounters and experiences and that I found his account fascinating and not hard to believe at all. James continued, "Uncle Roy died in the same back field, you know. He had a sudden massive heart attack and was dead when I found him several minutes later. We had him buried right and proper, and that should have been the end of it, according to most people. But two days later, I was just coming out the front door here when I saw a bright, glowing light shining over the house . . . oh, about 50 feet right out from where we are standing right now. It was just getting to be sunset, and at first I told myself it was the sun. However, it landed right out there, where the front field meets the back field as it sort of winds around there. It landed, I tell you! And I swear to you that it was a small, saucer-shaped craft and not like anything our military has at all.

"It just came straight down and sat there for a while, still sort of glowing but not as much. It had a goldish-orange color to the glow. I didn't move off the porch but finally I did go down the steps and got to within about 40 feet. The hatch door opened and, I swear to you on my mother's grave, Uncle Roy stepped into the light from within the ship, at the very top of the hatch door, and waved to me. He didn't get out, mind you. He just waved once, real friendly like. I got the feeling in my heart that he was saying he was happy now. He was finally with his friends . . ."

James stopped talking for a moment, hesitated, and then went on. "These were the friends he kept telling me about who he met in the field in his younger days. You know, I saw them too. And now I wait for them – just like Uncle Roy did!"

This case is but a single example of several the authors know of in which persons who have died have later been seen aboard a UFO, happily at home with the crew and traveling presumably among the stars. We must be careful here, however, and not jump to any hasty conclusions. We can't assume for a moment that all UFO occupants previously lived on earth and are now freely roaming the heavens in the afterlife.

From our study of metaphysics, what seems to be happening is that, upon his passing, Uncle Roy's soul moved from our dimension frequency into a heavenly frequency which he chose before his passing, though he might not have been conscious of what he was doing. His constant dwelling on UFOs and the friendly space folk he met drew his soul to their dimension since they were operating on the same frequency.

It would be apparent, to our thinking at least, that if you believe strongly enough in extraterrestrial beings and feel that you are one with them, that when your time comes to "cross-over" from this plane to another, you might wind up where you feel the most at home.

Remember, the authors have studied UFOs for many years (having had personal experiences ourselves, enough to fill several books), and we realize fully well that a good percentage of the beings who are onboard these craft are much more spiritually evolved than we earthlings are. The space brothers, as we lovingly call them, have learned to lift their consciousness and their vibrations so that they have become ethereal and not physical in composition.

A good friend of ours whom we mentioned previously, Gabriel Green of Yucca Valley, California, is very happy today even though his charming, much beloved wife is no longer with him in a physical sense. Gabe knows that she is able to communicate with him from her rather lofty position aboard a large mothership that hangs invisible over the California desert, sending down loving vibrations in an attempt to lift the consciousness of the population of the West Coast. As we shall see in the following chapter, the space people have a definite purpose in making themselves known at this time. Their appearance has to do with the physical death of the Planet; a world that is much like we humans who inhabit it in that it has a spirit and a soul which will continue to live on, even if the world itself should be destroyed.

WILL EARTH MERGE WITH THE HEAVENS IN THE NEW AGE?

Great physical, mental and spiritual changes are taking place on earth and will continue to do so as we progress onward in the new millennium. These changes – some of which will be disastrous – will effect each and every one of us, both positively and negatively. The earth will rumble with earthquakes and volcanic activity, the weather will shift drastically, entire continents will rise while others will sink into the sea in the twinkling of an eye.

Every psychic, every UFO contactee and every spiritual leader from Billy Graham on see "great changes" in the months and years just ahead. And now, even those reporting near-death-experiences are coming forward to tell of their being able to peer into the future and witness the upheaval that is to strike. What all these same "awakened" individuals also report observing from their lofty perch out of the physical body is a New Age, or Golden Age which will come immediately after this period of strife.

Dr. Kenneth Ring, mentioned earlier in this volume for his research into afterlife phenomena, has recently updated his findings in a book titled "Heading Toward Omega." In his new work, published by William Morrow, Dr. Ring once again interviewed patients who had "died" and come back to life. Many of those he spoke with trembled as they told him of a future in which humankind would live in peace and would prosper and that mankind would be one with nature and with God.

Dr. Ring's patients spoke of harmony and universal brotherhood and a spiritual awakening like none that has gone before. My own contacts with interdimensional beings would lead me to believe that, while there is great turmoil ahead for us, eventually the wicked will perish through their own deeds, and those of goodness and light will progress to unheralded heights and will go on to live in a truly "Golden Age" of abundance, good health, enhanced psychic powers and a knowledge of God's role in their everyday lives.

During this period of turmoil, many whose vibrations remain pure will be lifted from this planet in spaceships and will be housed in great motherships or satellite cities which are now in orbit around our planet but which remain invisible as they exist in higher realms as of the present time. Evidently, the new millennium holds something special for the human race. Some feel that this is a wonderful time in which the heavenly dimensions and our physical state of being will merge and start to work in unison.

At that point, many of us will possess enhanced powers of extrasensory perception and will be able to travel from dimension to dimension without difficulty in craft which we will be able to power with our minds. This is the same period when Jesus will return and we, along with the Son of God, will be taken into the heavens. If you are a stickler for Biblical confirmation, remember that Elijah was taken up into heaven in a "chariot of fire . . . by a whirlwind." Later the same prophet was seen along with Moses at the Transfiguration as Jesus stood ready to travel skyward, His robe shining so brilliantly that it resembled the sun.

If Elijah could ascend to heaven without dying, it's entirely possible that many of us – or our whole planet – will find ourselves transported there in this New Age so many have prophesied will come.

THE GREAT BATTLE AND A REJOICING

According to religious scholars, before this golden time of peace there will, however, be a great battle in which the forces of good – the Christ forces – will combat the forces of evil led by the mighty Satan. A fierce, fever-pitched battle will be waged in which all sorts of science fiction-like weapons will be used to engulf the planet, and everyone still alive on it, in a literal ball of fire.

Millions – no, billions – will be incinerated as God judges our worth and prepares to cleanse the planet so that "a new heaven and a new earth" can be built from the ashes. Those that have been taken from the Planet will be returned to find a glorious kingdom as described by John in the "New International Version" of the Bible: "I saw a new heaven and a new earth, for the first heaven and the first earth has passed away, and there was no longer any sea. I saw the Holy City, the New Jerusalem, coming down out of heaven from God, prepared as a bride beautifully dressed for her husband. And I heard a loud voice from the throne saying, 'Now the dwelling of God is with men, and He will live with them. They will be His people, and God Himself will be with them and be their God. He will wipe every tear from their eyes. There will be no more death or mourning or crying or pain, for the old order of things has passed away.'"

Now if God is not talking about a merging of dimensions, a blending of our physical realm with heaven, then what is He speaking of? It seems to me that the meaning of Revelations is as clear as the nose on your face and can hardly be interpreted in any other fashion. The reason why those who have passed on have been seen onboard UFOs now becomes more evident. The operators of these shining neon lights are not of the physical, but exist in higher, more heavenly realms and dimensions.

Because of their advanced spiritual state they no longer have to dwell in physical bodies but can take on any appearance that they so choose. Many of the aliens that have been encountered may look remarkably humanoid in appearance, but that is because they can disguise themselves so as not to frighten those they contact. Their true essence is pure light and they, like the strangers of the scriptures, can travel the universe and be anywhere instantaneously, whether it be on earth in a farmer's field or in God's heavenly realms.

After we have died they can "pick up" certain souls whose mission has been accomplished on earth in the physical sense and who are ready to go on to more celestial things.

GLORIA LEE AND THE SPACE BROTHERS

The late Gloria Lee was a very attractive woman in her mid-thirties who rode the skies as a stewardess for one of the major airlines. In her off duty hours, Gloria had another loftier side to her personality. Claiming to have met spiritually advanced beings from other worlds, Gloria would meditate for hours on end, during which time these entities of cosmic good will would channel messages through her. Much of what they had to say has been retained in a small spiral bound volume titled *"Why We Are Here"* (available from Inner Light Publications for $10.95).

Several of the discourses confirm this impending merger of earth with the heavens as well as explaining further the nature of spiritual beings said to exist throughout this solar system and others.

"The world we live in is physical in a sense," Gloria's alien friend stated. "Perhaps not to you, for your eyes cannot see us. The world we live in is etheric and is in the higher ethers of the physical plane. Your science knows only the three lower ethers. We exist in the four higher ethers, but also reside in the three lower as our plane of life encompasses the whole."

As for the coming New Age, the interdimensional being went on thusly: "In your Golden Age, love will reign supreme, the same brotherly love your teachers wanted so much to teach you through the ages. Now, this will become a reality. You will easily feel what you should towards each other in this Christ vibration.

"Gradually this will become stronger and stronger. In time, your planet will raise itself out of this lower physical and become one with us. Then all the solar system will rejoice as brothers in love with God. To you, our worlds would be the most wonderful you could see. The worlds we see in all the universe have not been as inharmonious as yours. The planets in our solar system will once again be in harmony when your planet moves into a higher vibration. Then you will really begin to see what a difference this will make to your civilization."

Other space contacts have espoused pretty much the same sort of cosmic philosophy, regardless if the person being contacted lives in America, China, Brazil or Africa. Indeed, there seems to be an overall universality in the majority of these communications from more advanced beings.

THE CASE OF PAULINE SHARP

"I asked when the great holocaust was to come. The spirit force showed me.

"As the years rolled past, the light above became brighter and stronger. I saw a black cloud cover the earth so thickly that nothing could be seen. This would be the fulfillment of the prophecy concerning the three days and three nights of darkness that would envelop the planet, occurring through the grace of our merciful God. It would be when the two realms, the third and the fourth dimensions, already increasingly intermingling, would merge so that man on earth would be able to see many forms of fourth dimensional life. But it would be too much for most people to see this all at once, and so the darkness to permit gradual adaptation. Then a sunburst will shake the entire western hemisphere.

"Finally, when the Aquarian Age has become fully operative, each planet revolving around the sun of our solar system will rotate at a different rate than presently, thus changing the length of days on each planet. The day of earth will be closer to twenty-eight and one-half hours."

This vision is but one of many hundreds regarding future land changes and prophecies which have come through Pauline Sharp, who respectfully requests that she be addressed by her spiritual name, Yolanda. Before her abilities became more pronounced to receive messages from evolved, super, non-physical beings, Yolanda was a successful businesswoman.

Today, she heads an international society which promotes world peace and brotherhood. Mark Age Associations (Box 290388, Ft. Lauderdale, FL 33329) publishes news and information in preparation for what they say is the Second Coming and the New Age of Aquarius.

"We are now," Yolanda states confidently, "in the final cleansing period, preparatory to the much discussed Golden Age." This is the long-prophesied "Harvest Period," the age when she says all error will be swept from earth and from the minds of those men who would remain as they are now.

"For the earth, and all on it, are even now in the process of being transmuted, raised to a higher vibration. We are now entering the Fourth Dimension, wherein all that exists on earth, and the earth itself, will exist in a higher state of evolution."

There will be, and, according to Yolanda, are even now in process many changes in all forms of life. It is to be considered "a natural step in the evolutionary progress of a planet and will take place regardless of life existing on it." The many and varied earth changes already in effect, as well as the weather patterns and other related phases, are but small examples of how the entire earth is to be changed for this "Aquarian Age."

"These changes," according to Yolanda, "are increasingly evident in man himself. They have brought many to the realization that there is a need for a vast change taking place these days. Body structures are being affected. New and impossible-to-diagnose ailments (such as AIDS) and body conditions are perplexing nearly everyone. These are due to the vibrational changes, and to what each one is, or is not, doing about them."

Also, in this New Age period, many are having "strange mental and psychic experiences, keeping them secret in fear that others will classify them as unbalanced, neurotic or hysterical. But those who know the causes and work with the changes are experiencing dramatic favorable results. Those who do not understand them, or will not act accordingly when they do know, are going through many painful trials."

Yolanda points out that the Bible tells us, "The old men will have dreams and the young men will have visions and they will prophesy the ending of an age."

Hundreds of thousands of persons all over the world, Yolanda claims, are having an outpouring of this Spirit, "and it is increasing rapidly and dramatically all the time. This is the age of marks, in which many varied signs of the times alert man to the fact that it is indeed the latter-day or the Mark-Age period." While many have kept quiet about their unusual experiences and demonstrations of spiritual talents, now many are telling of them. In the prophecies concerning the coming cataclysms, Yolanda is quick to point out, nowhere is mention made of the end of the world.

Instead, she foresees numerous cataclysms throughout the world "as the planet and all on it are transmuted into the higher frequency vibration of the fourth dimension. Nor are all these cataclysms to be purely physical but many are to take mental and emotional forms."

The reason for these changes, Yolanda explains is to cleanse and to prepare the planet for the New or Golden Age which already has dawned. There have been, and are to be, those earth changes necessary to renew the land or to furnish new lands for the coming era. However, many of even these, and certainly all of the mental and emotional cataclysms, would not have been necessary had man here risen into his spiritual consciousness.

For then he would have known this is a preordained evolvement for this planet, preparatory to one for the entire solar system, and would have known and would have been told how to make the change properly. Also, he would not have created the tremendous errors which have to be cleansed, both within himself and the nature kingdoms.

Looking around us, we see many signs that man is awakening from a cosmic sleep or dream of thousands of years' duration. When Tim and I first got involved in this field, many of the aspects of what can loosely be defined as New Age beliefs, and which are now pretty much accepted, were put down by those still in a state of slumber. Few people, for example, believed that a person's health could be positively affected by the food that they ate.

You were a weirdo or, at best, a faddist, if you were into not eating meat. Vitamins were thought to have no beneficial value, and exercise was only for athletes until Jane Fonda and Richard Simmons made aerobics, doing sit-ups, and yoga an enjoyable experience that anyone could participate in by watching early morning television.

Today, thanks to Shirley MacLaine's best seller "Out On A Limb," you don't automatically get locked up if you express a belief in reincarnation, UFOs and healthful living. It is not just by "coincidence" that such subjects are now being brought into the open.

The residents of higher dimensions and of the heavenly realms are trying to awaken us spiritually as they know of the changes in vibration and density that will soon be changing our lives. They want us to be ready for these events so that we will not be swept away in the tide of negativity that has encircled our earth like a dense cloud for centuries. Yes, there will be a blending of dimensions, and it will be a great day like no other in the history of humankind.

ELECTRONIC TRANSMISSIONS FROM THE SPIRIT REALMS

Mark Macy is the head of the INIT-US, which stands for the International Network for Instrumental Transcommunication, a group of researchers cooperating under an ethical umbrella to bring the public up to the minute data provided by residents of the spirit realms via telephone, TV signal, computer and other electronic means.

In fact, Macy maintains that engineers operating from other realms and dimensions who once resided here on the Earth are now working together from the "other side" to provide us with the necessary evidence via up-to-the-minute electronic transmissions that death is not the end of our existence as individual spiritual souls.

Apparently, any number of broadcasts have been made to date from this dimension alongside our own, and physical apports have even "come through" a kind of screen door that separates our world from the "hereafter."

The following article is reprinted from "Psychic News," Britain's oldest and most respected spiritual publication, and details the INIT's work with Macy at the helm. Mark says that he is convinced that "many people are looking in the wrong direction for intelligent life beyond Earth; rather than outward into the physical universe, we'd have better luck looking inward into subtler dimensions that exist all around us all the time."

Readers who are interested in furthering their knowledge of this form of communication with heavenly realms may contact the INIT directly at Box 11036, Boulder, CO 80301, and request information on their publications, which include the book "Conversations Beyond the Light."

My country's two main media exports this year have been the O. J. Simpson trial and the glossy TV series, "Baywatch" (also known as "Babe-watch"), leaving the impression that much of the world views life in the USA as something of a circus.

So I wish to thank "Psychic News" and its editor Tim Haugh for this opportunity to spread the word of instrumental transcommunication (ITC) in a good light. Hopefully this report on some rather exciting and serious research will help in its own small way to offset the balance of the more sensational media.

A BRIEF OVERVIEW OF INSTRUMENTAL TRANSCOMMUNICATION

Most readers of "Psychic News" are familiar with research into the electronic voice phenomenon which has been under way since the 1950s in Europe, the USA and elsewhere. Experimenters have been finding very weak voices on their audio tapes lasting one to two seconds. In the 1980s, things began to happen which indicated that the research was becoming less of a voice phenomenon and more of a means of conveying significant information in the form of text, voices and pictures from the worlds of spirit to Earth.

Klaus Schreiber, a German experimenter with strong psychic skills, received instructions from his invisible friends to turn on the TV to an empty channel and aim a video camera at the set. The result was a picture of his deceased daughter Karin. Soon he was receiving other paranormal images, including a picture purported to be that of the great scientist, Albert Einstein, with whom Schreiber claimed to be in telepathic contact.

After Schrieber's death in 1986, he began assisting his earth-side colleagues from the other side of the veil. In the summer of 1990, experimenters received two pictures in their computer, one of Schreiber himself and the other of his new home in the astral worlds.

The messages accompanying the pictures said: "Klaus S. as we all know him but now in a new world. These pictures are from Klaus. One shows the house in which he now lives together with his family members.

"For months of earth time, Klaus was on a path of investigating his surroundings. Many new arrivals make up for what they could not complete on Earth. Klaus is again experimenting with picture transmission and sends out pictures at random in the hope that his friends on Earth will receive them."

In 1985, Maggy and Jules Harsch-Fishbach began their experiments in Luxembourg, and they soon built up the interdimensional support with deceased ITC pioneer Konstantin Raudive. He had joined a spirit group calling itself "Timestream," which was being assembled with the intent of ushering in a new generation of contacts between "heaven" and earth.

In the autumn of 1986, a new voice joined the sessions. It was a high-pitched, computer-like voice that was almost too perfect to be human. During one session, the group asked a question about God, and the high-pitched voice interrupted: "Please address this question to me." And Maggy asked, "Who exactly ARE you?"

Came the reply: "We are what we are. It is not easy to explain to you. I am not an energy being, not a light being. I was never human, never an animal, and was never incarnate. Neither am I God!

"You are familiar with the popular picture of two children walking across a bridge. Behind them is a being that protects them. This is what I am to you but without wings. If you insist on giving me a name, call me Technician."

As months passed, Technician astounded the researchers with his exceptional knowledge of electronics, physics, mathematics, astronomy, general science, history and the future. He had a memory like a living computer and spoke many languages. Here is one message that came from Technician: "Fear of death is one of the most distressing concepts of human culture. It is based on the conscious belief that your bodily existence offers life and security, which it never wants to lose.

"Fear of death, therefore, is evidence of the mind having lost its roots. It shows a spiritual being who has far removed itself from its higher self.

"You owe this mentality largely to an intellectual and scientific way of thinking. It wants all thoughts reduced to a comprehensible level of material existence.

"Heaven is in man and those who have heaven within themselves go to heaven. Heaven is in all those who recognize what is of God and let themselves be guided by the Divine. This priority, and the basic concern of every religion, has always been the acknowledgement of God!"

Since then, Technician has played a key role in the unfoldment of ITC on earth, always careful to stay in the background while directing and protecting the human experimenters on both sides of the veil. Without the involvement of Technician and other higher beings in the project, ITC would not be advancing as quickly nor as safely as it is today. This all sounds a bit absurd to many people today, but is it really?

HOW DOES ITC WORK?

A decade of careful, well-documented experiments and many helpful hints from our invisible colleagues have given us an emerging picture of a reality that is quite alien to modern, civilized man. Before understanding the inner workings of ITC, a person must first understand this broadened view of life. Not necessarily accept it (as it may rub against some very sacred, very personal beliefs) but at least understand it.

Over the years, mystics of the East, science fiction writers and parapsychologists of the West have offered glimpses of this strange reality to a public and

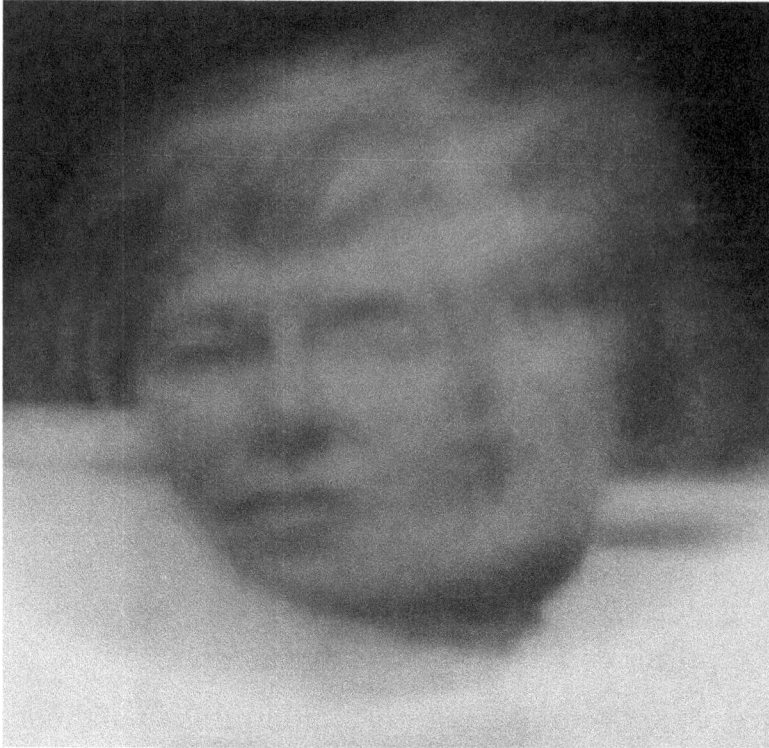

Phantom photos appear from the other side in experiments conducted by Mark Macy of INIT-US. The faces of the spirits superimpose themselves upon the distorted images of the living.

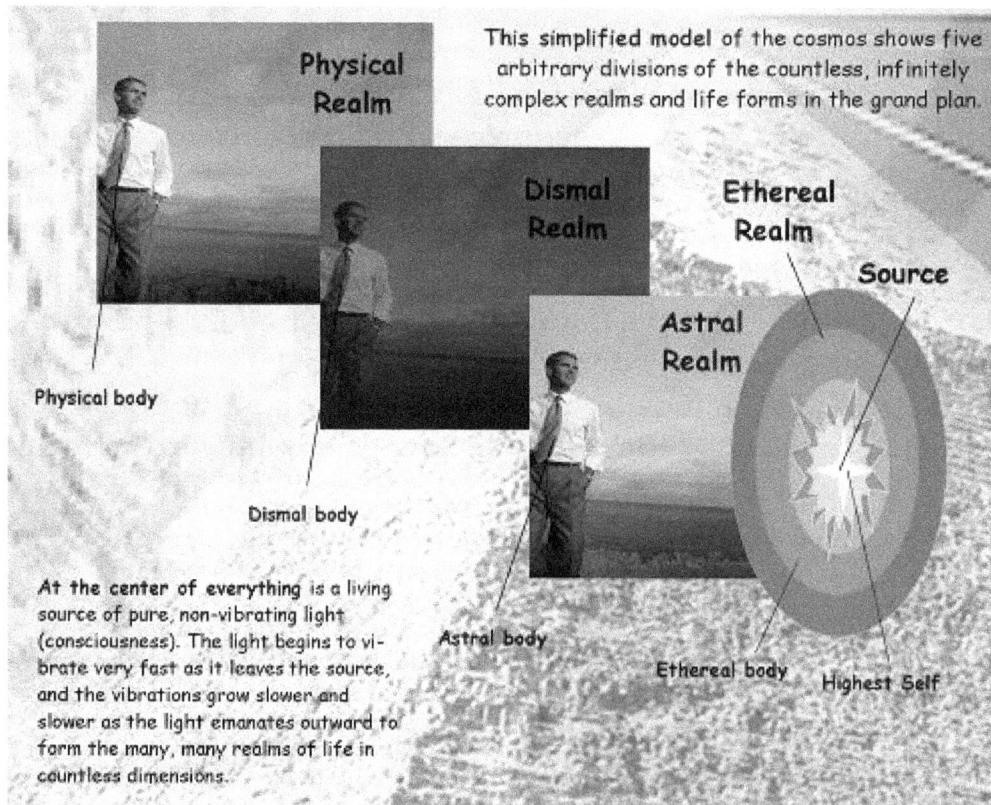

This simplified model of the cosmos shows five arbitrary divisions of the countless, infinitely complex realms and life forms in the grand plan.

Physical Realm

Dismal Realm

Ethereal Realm

Source

Astral Realm

Physical body

Dismal body

Astral body

Ethereal body

Highest Self

At the center of everything is a living source of pure, non-vibrating light (consciousness). The light begins to vibrate very fast as it leaves the source, and the vibrations grow slower and slower as the light emanates outward to form the many, many realms of life in countless dimensions.

The World(s) of spirit according to INIT-US via Mark Macy - www.http://macyafterlife.com/

a scientific establishment that has remained largely skeptical. They tell us stories of people dematerializing from one spot and rematerializing elsewhere; of people overcoming gravity, causing their bodies to rise. They talk of invisible dimensions, teeming with life, superimposed over our own physical plane. Stories are told of material objects made to move or change with thoughts. Others speak of mystics emitting a flow of oil or a tailing of ash from the palms of their hands, of large, disc-shaped objects appearing mysteriously in the sky, then blinking out.

Cases arise of people projecting their mental images onto photographic film. There are haunted houses, spirit possessions, apports. And now comes ITC, the use of electronic equipment to get long messages and clear images from the invisible worlds of spirit.

For those businessmen, bankers, laborers and engineers alive on Earth today who wish to keep both feet planted firmly on the ground, it is most effective simply to draw a line between themselves and all of these phenomena. It can be very unsettling to venture across that line into the tangled jungle of otherworldly situations.

Why is it unsettling? For one thing, as we look beyond that line, we begin to realize that life is rather complex. Our physical universe seems to be superimposed on other universes, like radio and TV signals that are all jumbled together in the same room. And like these signals, each universe or dimension has its own laws due to its frequency or vibratory rate.

So, in the quest for extraterrestrial life, we realize that our astronomers may be looking in the wrong direction; instead of outward to the stars, perhaps they should be looking inward into subtler dimensions that exist right here, all around us.

Other sciences are also looking the wrong way in many cases, and that is not reassuring. As we cross the line into the paranormal, our sense of linear time – past present and future – begins to fade away. So, when we talk of reincarnation, we are no longer talking of past lives and future lives but of concurrent lives.

In the spirit worlds, or subtler dimensions, we are told that everything unfolds at once into a multidimensional panorama in a way that is impossible for most people on Earth to fathom. Our sense of distance fades away. Space, like time, is said to be a fleeting aberration of the physical dimension. An illusion.

Someday, we are told, we will indeed have vehicles that "fade away" into a subtler dimension, move as quickly as thought and "fade back" into the physical realm, perhaps at a destination many light-years away from the point of departure. As we cross the line into the paranormal, the very ground on which we walk – as solid as it seems – begins to fade away into the illusion (which Hindus have

159

warned us for thousands of years it really is!).

That, dear readers, begins to set up a framework in which we can begin to understand the inner workings of ITC. It would be nice if we could just turn on a TV, computer or radio, or pick up the telephone, and get messages and images from the spirit worlds, but unfortunately it's not that simple. In fact, ITC success depends on some rather complex variables.

In July, I visited my friends the Harsch-Fishbachs in Luxembourg. We sat around a configuration of radios and received a long message from Konstantin Raudive. As the hissing white noise of the radios faded out, Dr. Raudive's voice faded in. His first statement was this: "It can only work when the vibrations of those present are in complete harmony and when their aims and intentions are pure."

And another comment made more recently, again, in Luxembourg: "Dear friends, as you have already been told by the Technician, should we not be able to anchor transcommunication in this century it will most certainly happen in the next one. An apparatus will be functioning when unity of mind is achieved among researchers. Each of us is responsible for ourselves. This is Konstantin Raudive."

So, that seems to be one of the ITC puzzle pieces. There must be harmony, pure intentions and unity of mind among experimenters before ITC can work. The following statement by Swejen Salter might provide the second piece of the puzzle: "We regret that there are not more stable ITC bridges, but the contact field of the experimenter contributes most to this. It is the very reason why we cannot reach some individuals through radio, TV or computer. Your linear thinking makes contacts more difficult to us and with us."

Our spirit colleagues encourage us to move our minds into a more timeless reality, a quality that seems to be closely associated with what we typically call "psychic skills."

So, from these messages, I would conclude the following: An ITC works best when it involves a group of psychically sensitive people whose vibrations are in complete harmony and whose aims and intentions are pure. It does not work so well when it involves one good psychic with his or her equipment. ITC does not work with a group of great psychics who are jealous or resentful of each other, because jealousy, resentment and other such feelings create static that disrupts all communications across dimensions. So does hostile skepticism. I am beginning to realize that ITC does not involve an individual here on Earth communicating with a person in the spirit world, although that's the way it may seem to us today.

I think it is really a group of people on Earth working with a team of spirit beings, and they are all in one mind. They all feel and live that openness. The ITC experimenters, their supporters, their spirit colleagues, and all the equipment on both sides of the veil are all part of a single system. They are one.

When that situation becomes widespread, I believe we will start seeing good ITC contacts around the world on a regular basis. We do know that the hardware or equipment involved in ITC is a very minor consideration for ITC work today. The experimenters who concentrate purely on the technical of ITC are getting the poorest results. Those who take the time to nurture ties with their friends, loved ones and colleagues in the spirit world are those who are attracting capable help from the Other Side. And make no mistake. At the present time all the technology for advanced ITC contacts is being assembled on the other side of the veil, not here on Earth.

That will certainly change in the future, but for the time being we lack the technologies that deal with life energies. I'm talking about equipment that reacts to our thoughts and attitudes. Meanwhile, the best we on Earth can do to facilitate the spread of ITC is to be aware of and nurture the contact field. This is a field of life energy (chi, shakti, psi, subtle energy, cosmic energy, Holy Spirit, etc.) that is automatically formed whenever two or more beings develop an awareness of each other.

It is formed on our attitudes, thoughts, beliefs and feelings. In ITC, a strong contact field is built over time between a team of experimenters on Earth and a team of spirit colleagues. It is this interdimensional energy field that acts as a sort of etheric power supply to make ITC contacts possible.

But enough of this technical information. I'll continue this article with some of the recent contacts my colleagues in Luxembourg have received.

THE LATEST ITC EVIDENCE

As more people inform themselves about ITC and new contacts are experienced worldwide, the phenomenon continues to grow. Last year saw a spread of ITC telephone contacts beyond Europe. On January 14 of last year, I received a phone call from our spirit colleague Konstantin Raudive announcing the creation of a new ITC bridge to the US. A week later, my colleague, ITC pioneer George Meek, received a call at his home. On the same day, researchers Sarah Estep and Walter Uphoff were called by Raudive, and, a few weeks later, Hans Heckmann got a call.

Within three months, more than a dozen calls were reported by the five of us in the States. Our colleagues in Brazil and Sweden also began to receive calls from Konstantin Raudive announcing the spread of ITC bridges. Before long, accusations of a hoax began to surface. After all, such contacts made across public networks could easily be faked. The accusations came not from the scientific community, as one might guess, but from within the ranks. Several longtime voice experimenters in Germany and the USA, who have never received such long, clear messages, just would not believe that they were legitimate despite independent confirmations of these international, interdimensional calls at other receiving stations.

One such confirmation came on February 20, a month after the first call to the States. German researcher Adolf Homes received a computer message: "Dear Colleague Adolf Homes. I herewith confirm my own contacts with Mr. Malkhoff (in Germany) and Mr. Meek and Mr. Macy in America

"More contacts have been made successfully in China and Japan by telephone and fax. Our tests are necessary because humanity is in a state of being – created by itself – which is negative for us to the point that we cannot influence consciousness.

"We therefore ask you to encourage people to open their psychic barriers to a greater extent. Only then is there a chance for us to continue contacts via radio receivers, televisions and computers.

"Unfortunately, messages from our side by telephone and fax do not suffice to make clear to humanity our reality as one of many realities. This is Konstantin Raudive."

Homes' computer was and is hooked up to nothing but the power outlet in the wall. No modems or networks. So unless Homes himself were perpetrating an elaborate hoax, his computer message from Raudive is good, solid evidence for the legitimacy of the phone calls. All colleagues of Adolf Homes know him to be an honest, serious researcher.

Then, as soon as the phone calls began to stir up excitement, they ended just as abruptly. Our colleague in Brazil, Sonia Rinaldi, received a phone call from Konstantin Raudive late last month; but otherwise the lines everywhere have been still. Except, of course, in the main experimental stations in Luxembourg and Germany, which continue to get contacts of various kinds on a regular basis. The Luxembourg experimenters have been told several times during recent contacts that ITC is presently entering a new phase. During this phase, the people interested in ITC will be given time to digest the information already received.

How they come to feel about ITC will determine how Spirit will proceed in the future. On December 17 last year, Konstantin Raudive confirmed this through an equipment configuration in Luxembourg called Burton-Bridge II: "The continuation of the project will be decided by higher beings.

"They currently observe the attitudes and reactions of people concerning ITC. You can look at it as sort of a higher discussion. These discussions have been going on since 1994 your time. These higher beings do not know earth time. A few minutes of discussion on our side may be comparable to months or even years on earth. If these beings give me permission, I will announce myself again by the same means."

The impression I'm getting from all this is that there is some serious concern among higher beings over the state and fate of the planet. I believe they see great power in ITC as a means of shaping our destiny, and they are trying to see that the power is not misused in its early stages. Incidentally, before I became involved in ITC, I didn't even believe in the existence of higher beings. Now I have no doubts whatsoever, but that is a story in itself, and I do not wish to digress from the focus of this article. If all this is still a stretch for you, please bear with me.

APPORTS SINCE 1992

Maggy and Jules Harsh-Fishbach of Luxembourg have received apports – the materialization of physical objects – from time to time in addition to the text, voices and pictures they receive on a more regular basis.

I will discuss them only briefly, as physical objects mean less to me than insights. Our physical world has countless objects scattered about, but fewer good ideas that can raise the love and wisdom quotient (just my opinion, of course).

First apport. My Luxembourg friends like to relax by traveling to old fortresses and castles and studying history. In the spring of 1993, they visited a museum in Virton, Belgium, which unfortunately was closed, and when returning to the empty parking lot, found an old Luxembourg coin next to the car. They were reasonably certain that it had not been there when they had arrived.

Second apport. In April last year, while visiting the fortress Bollen-dorf in Germany, suddenly in the air, about five yards above them, a small, bright object seemed to form. It rotated with great speed and spun around its own axis. The object, because of its rapid spin, seemed to stay in the air for a few moments and then fell at their feet with a clinking sound. The coin was warm to the touch, and there was no one around. One side of the coin carried the inscription, "LUDOV XVI. D. GRATIA." On the other side was a coat of arms with three lilies and the inscription, "1791 FRANCAIE ET NAVARRAE REX." The next day, Jules and Maggy found the following paranormal text in their computer: "Congratulations! You have found one end of the tunnel. At the other end is what you are looking for in the form of metal. You may look at the goal you reached yesterday as the final results of your trips and excursions.

"The second end will be the product of further development. Healings and your continuing path of life are connected with it, as everything is connected with each other and becomes one.

"Be guided by your inner-self and you will reach the goal. I preferred this apport to a voice contact and we advanced by it. I shall still call you next week at a good time for both of us. Will give the exact time on Monday. All my love and Tschuk, Swejen."

A few days later, Swejen told Maggy that the apport was a text from their side to practice the passage of objects through the "tunnel."

Swejen: "The coin is from the year 1791 during the reign of Louis XVI."

Maggy: "Have people helped with the experiment who lived during that time?"

Swejen: "Of course, they are the part of Group Timestream. Many became interested in ITC after you visited Varennes in autumn 1993."

Maggy: "Did the apports have to happen exactly at this place and at this point in time or could we have been somewhere else?"

Swejen: "It had to be this place at exactly this time. It is a place you have to drive to again before you will experience any more materializations."

Maggy: "Did we have to search further to the north or the south'?"

"Swejen: "I cannot tell you yet, but it was important at this time for you to be here. It was a test to activate the tunnel on both sides."

Maggy: "If I understand correctly, a similar method can also be used for the healing?"

Swejen: "Yes, exactly."

Maggy: "But apparently you cannot tell me anything more about that now."

Swejenz "Not now, we have to wait. But I can tell you that the moment when you were at one end of the tunnel where the apport could take place, we were able to make measurements and practically were able to make you visible as a hologram on our side."

Maggy: "Oh, really?"

Swejen: "We shall try something similar in the final phase of the healing process. We shall tell you more about it soon."

Third apport. A few days later, on April 29, the Harsch-Fishbachs drove to Larochette and visited the castle there. Nothing happened, so they walked to the terrace of a nearby hotel. When Maggy momentarily lifted her handbag off the table, there was an object on the table that was not there moments earlier. It was a thin, silver-colored coin with the inscription, "1702 LVD XIII D G FRETNAVARRAE."

Fourth apport. On May 11, the couple were sitting outside Falkenstein castle. Two old trees stood on either side of the bench. Suddenly there was a loud rustling in the branches, and an object dropped out of the leaves. Carefully, Jules spread apart the grass and found a golden bracelet. Arriving home at 11:15 PM, they found a message from experimenter Adolf Homes from Rivenich, Germany, on their telephone answering device. His deceased mother Elise Karoline had notified him that Maggy and Jules had found her bracelet which she lost under "mysterious circumstances" in the year 1933 near castle Falkenstein.

Nobody besides spirit colleague Swejen Salter had known about their trip to Falkenstein, so it was evidential indeed to receive this message from Adolf Homes upon arriving home. Homes is receiving regular contacts from his departed mother, Elise Karoline, by the same means by which Swejen Salter contacts the Luxembourg couple. Elise Karoline and Swejen have been cooperating regularly in the spirit world.

Maggy called Adolf Homes to confirm that they had found his mother's bracelet. The following morning, Maggy found a message from Elise Karoline Homes in her computer. It ran: "The bracelet is for you, Maggy. It is a gift from me. I shall notify my son. He is happy about it. Elise Karoline Homes."

Fifth apport. On May 15, the couple turned on the computer, and a small object dropped down from the ceiling, hit the keyboard and fell on the floor. They found a pendant in the shape of a face mask of white and gold color. Four days later they discovered a message on their computer which included a note from Swejen Salter: "The 'Peduccio' is from the Lombardian group."

Swejen explained that the name "Peduccio" referred to the apported gold pendant.

Sixth apport. On July 2, they visited the ruins of the fortress in Kronenburg, Germany, which once housed a "Commandment" of the Knights Templars. Near the entrance of the town they experienced the materialization of a gold pendant in the shape of a cross. On one side, a small ornament is engraved with a design; on the other side, the name "JERUSALEM" appears. A few days later, Konstantin Raudive came through on Burton-Bridge II: "The pendant came to you from the former French Knight Templar Airenet, who has joined Group Timestream."

Apparently Airenet had participated in the crusade to Jerusalem.

Seventh apport. On the evening of October 31 last year, Maggy and Jules set out for a place of pilgrimage in the south of Luxembourg. They arrived at 8:50

PM at a grotto which was cut out of rock. While they were still trying to interpret the inscription in the dark, a small metallic object "formed" itself above their heads and seemed to mix with the rain drops. The glittering object twirled across Maggy's right shoulder and came to rest before their feet. They picked it up and recognized a finely crafted golden pendant depicting the head of an eagle.

Eighth apport. Another gold pendant, bigger than the others, this time depicting a flying eagle, arriving in the Harsch-Fishbach apartment on the morning of December 17, 1994, while Maggy was busy with the care of their two parrots. The object seemed to fall off the ceiling. The parrots were excited and nervously flapped their wings. Maggy discovered text in the computer which announced a spirit group calling itself Group Eagle.

Swejen Salter later explained: "This is a new group. They deal mostly with the compression of objects of materialization. Lorenzo Tellarini, Umberto Ursi, and Cornelia Bandi are in charge. They hope you like the object."

CONTACTS

On November 10, last year, Maggy found a picture and letter in her computer. It ran as follows: "The entity who was called Anne Guigne during her lifetime and left Earth on January 14, 1922, showed herself on October 10 at 10:12 AM Via TV in Rivenich and through your scanner program in Luxembourg. Her message is as follows: 'As a little girl in France I got very ill. I was an important source of information. Through spiritual insight and prayer I learned from the omnipotence that I was better able to understand the things I needed to know here in the third level and could do more for mankind from here than on Earth.

"'I desired the change into a multidimensional world and was allowed a fast passing over to a world some memory of which was still alive in me. It is the same beautiful world you have heard about from others like me.

"'There are 35,000 to 40,000 children dying daily on earth. My task became clear to me. Together with other scientists, physicians and theologians, I am in charge of a group for the protection of all the newborn life. We are particularly concerned about those who have to die as children.

"'As you know, the conception of guilt does not exist here. However, we do not understand your overall attitude towards these entities who voluntarily walk the path of incarnation and are part of all that is.

"'In particular, it is your consciousness that bears the responsibility for your children, not only by evolutionary law but also by the natural laws of all that is.

"'Be aware therefore that the wars and violent events caused by you, and from which particularly your innocent children suffer, are not sparing you part of the so-called purgatory. Just the opposite.

"'Every debt you shoulder by sacrificing your own flesh and blood to wars is adding to the misery and suffering that awaits you.

"'The more you create your own hell on Earth by your criminal deeds and negligence, the less it will be diminished for you here later. Therefore consider carefully what you do.

"'We know that those among you who are actively pursuing ITC in a positive manner are not evil people. We want to encourage you to oppose crimes against the defenseless. You can do this by leading an honest life in accordance with spiritual cooperation.

"'Anne Guigne is greeting you, especially the children.'"

The following short message accompanied the picture:

"Anne Guigne. Born at Annecy on April 25, 1911. Transition made on January 14, 1922. Guardian angel of Remy."

In conclusion, it needs to be repeated that ITC today is at a crossroads. About the time this goes to press, more than a dozen top ITC researchers from throughout Europe and America will be converging on a meeting hall in the English countryside of Devon to help determine the future path of ITC. We are told by our spirit colleagues that the outcome of this meeting will have much to do with the spread of ITC in the coming years. For those of us who see ITC entwined with human destiny, it is not too great an exaggeration to say that we will be helping, in our own small way, to determine the fate of the planet.

Mark Macy, head of INIT-US (International Network for Instrumental Transcommunication.)

THE ELDER BIDS US FAREWELL

The dark veil has again fallen across the far fields of space, our Captain is dead, the precious cargoes of our lives are heaped, wasted and rotting, in the hold, and the astrolabe and compass are wrecked with the salt of twenty centuries.

Orion winks wickedly above, the Cobra has tumbled in six writhing rings at the feet of hapless Eve and the basket of forbidden berries that so troubled Eden is shrivelled and mouldy as hoarfrost. Cinderella has been rebuked by the fickle prince, Alice is imprisoned eternally in Underland, the Miracle is found to be a mirage, and Aladdin's lamp is lost forever.

How close we all come to dying, trapped in these little moments, these little unrelated vignettes, unaware of why we are here, oblivious of the journey, unconcerned about the destination. How close we come to dying before the reaper swoops down like the wrath of some mysterious, inscrutable, cruel Architect to wipe out everything. How hopelessly flawed are we that we are unable to see it or understand it or convey it to others.

It is now the hour which turns back the desire of the sailors, and melts their hearts; the hour they have said goodbye to their sweethearts and friends, and which pierces the heart of the mariner, if he hears from afar, the bell which seems to mourn the dying day.

Who can separate their faith from their actions, or their belief from their occupations? Who can spread their hours before them, saying, "This for my love and this for myself; this for my spirit and this other for my body"?

All your hours and days and years are but wings that beat through space and time from one self to another; from one birth to the next.

Whosoever wears their mortality as their best garment were better naked, for the wind and the sun will tear no holes in their skin.

And whosoever defines their conduct by ethics imprisons their song-bird in a cage, for the freest song comes not through bars and wires.

In reverie you cannot rise above your achievements nor fall lower than your failures. In adoration you cannot fly higher than your hopes nor humble yourself lower than your despair. And if you would know Peace, do not waste your days solving riddles.

Rather look about you and you shall see your love running and laughing with the children. Look into space; you shall see him hovering in the cloud, outstretching his arms in the lightning and descending in rain. You shall see him smiling in flowers, then rising and waving his hands in trees.

You would know the secret of death? But how shall you find it unless you seek it in the heart of life?

The owl whose night-bound eyes are blind unto the day cannot unveil the mystery of light. If you would indeed behold the spirit of death, open your heart wide unto the body of life, for life and death are one, even as the river and the sea are one.

In the depth of your hopes and desires lies your silent knowledge of the beyond; and like seeds dreaming beneath the snow your heart dreams of spring.

Trust the dreams, for in the dreams is hidden the gate to eternity.

What is it to die but to stand naked in the wind and to melt into the sun? And what is it to cease breathing but to free the breath from its restless tides, that it may rise and expand and seek Joy unencumbered?

Only when you drink from the river of silence shall you indeed sing, and when you have reached the mountain top, then you shall begin to climb, and when the earth shall claim your limbs, then shall you truly dance in the light.

Now it is evening, and Eva said, "It is a glorious day for your spirit has come to me and spoken."

And the Avatar answered, "Was it I alone who spoke? Did I not also listen?"

Then he descended the steps to the river Lethe and all his comrades and friends followed him.

And he reached his ship and stood upon the deck, and facing the friends again, he raised his voice and said: "People of Earth, the wind bids me leave you. Less hasty am I than the wind, yet I must go. We wanderers, ever seeking the lonelier way, begin no day where we have ended another day; and no sunrise finds us where sunset left us. Even while the earth sleeps we travel. We are the seeds of the tenacious plant, and it is in our ripeness and our fullness of heart that we are given to the wind and are scattered.

"My days among you were brief, and briefer still the words I have spoken. But should my voice fade in your ears, and my love vanish in your memory, then I will come again, and with a richer heart and lips more yielding to the spirit will I speak. Yes, I shall return with the tide, and though death may hide me, and the greater silence enfold me, yet again will I seek your under standing.

"I go with the wind, friends of Earth, but not down into emptiness; and if this day is not a fulfillment of your needs and my love, then let it be a promise 'til another day. Know, therefore, that from the great silence I shall return.

"The mist that drifts away at dawn, leaving but dew in the fields, shall rise and gather into a cloud and fall as rain, and not unlike the mist have I been. In the stillness of the night I have walked in your streets, and my spirit has entered your houses, and your heart-beats were in my heart, and your breath was upon my face, and I knew you all.

"Aye, I knew your joy and your pain, and in your sleep your dreams were my dreams, and oftentimes I was among you as a lake among the mountains. I mirrored the summits in you

169

and the bending slopes, and even the passing flocks of your thoughts and your desires. And to my silence came the laughter of your childhood, and the longing of your youth. And when they reached my depth the streams and the rivers were singing still.

"But sweeter still than laughter and greater than all longing, you, my love, my Eva, are boundless in me, and in beholding all these things of Earth I beheld you and loved you. For what distances can love reach that are not in that vast sphere? What visions, what expectations and what presumptions can outsoar that flight?

"And though this heavy-grounded ship awaits the tide upon these shores, yet, even like an ocean, we can neither hasten our tides nor wish them away. And like the seasons we are also, and though in our winter we deny our spring, yet spring, reposing within, smiles in her drowsiness and is not offended.

Think not I say these things in order that you may say the one to the other, "He praised us well. He saw but the good in us."

"I only speak to you in words of that which you yourselves know in thought.

"I have found that which is greater than wisdom. It is a flame spirit in you ever gathering more of itself, while you, heedless of its expansion, bewail the withering of your days. It is life in quest of life in bodies that fear the grave.

"But, my darling rosebud, there are no graves on yonder shore. These mountains and plains are a cradle and a stepping-stone. Whenever you pass by the field where you have laid your ancestors look deeply therein, and you shall see yourselves and your children dancing hand in hand.

"Less than a promise have I given, perhaps, and yet more generous have you been to me. You have given me my deeper thirsting after life.

"Surely there is no greater gift to a man than that which turns all his aims into reality and all life into a fountain. And in this lies my honour and my reward,— That whenever I come to the fountain to drink I find the living water itself thirsty; And it drinks me while I drink it.

"You are not enclosed within your bodies, nor confined to houses or fields. That which is you dwells above the mountain and roves with the wind. It is not a thing that crawls into the sun for warmth or digs holes into darkness for safety, but a thing free, a spirit that envelops the earth and moves in the ether.

"If these be vague words, then seek not to clear them. Vague and nebulous is the beginning of all things, but not their end, and I would have you remember me as a beginning. Life, and all that lives, is conceived in the mist and not in the crystal. And who knows but a crystal is mist in decay?

"This would I have you remember in remembering me:

"That which seems most gentle and bewildered in you is the strongest and most determined. Is it not your breath that has erected and hardened the structure of your bones? And is it not a dream which none of you remember having dreamt, that built your city and fashioned all there is in it? Could you but see the tides of that breath you would cease to see all else, and if you could hear the whispering of the dream you would hear no other sound.

170

"But you do not see, nor do you hear, and it is well. The veil that clouds your eyes shall be lifted by the hands that wove it, and the clay that fills your ears shall be pierced by those fingers that kneaded it.

"And one day you shall see. And one day you shall hear.

"Yet you shall not deplore having known blindness, nor regret having been deaf. For in that day you shall know the hidden purposes in all things, and you shall bless darkness as you would bless the light."

After saying these things he looked about him, and he saw Charon, the pilot of his ship, standing by the helm and gazing now at the full sails and now at the distance.

And he said:

"Ah, patient, ever patient, is the captain of my ship. The wind blows, and the sails are restless; even the rudder begs direction; yet quietly my captain awaits my silence. And these my mariners, who have heard the choir of the greater sea, they too have heard me patiently. Now they shall wait no longer. I am ready.

"The river has reached the sea, and once more the great mother holds her son against her breast. Fare you well, people of Earth. This day has ended. It is closing upon us even as the water-lily upon its own tomorrow. What was given us here we shall keep, and if it suffices not, then again must we come together and together stretch our hands unto the giver. Forget not that I shall come back to you.

"A little while, and my longing shall gather dust and foam for another body. A little while, my darling rosebud, a little while longer; a moment of rest upon the wind, and another woman shall bear me.

"Farewell to you and the youth I have spent with you. It was but yesterday we met in a dream. You have sung to me in my aloneness, and I of your longings have built a tower in the sky. But now our sleep has fled and our dream is over, and it is no longer dawn. The noontide is upon us and our half waking has turned to fuller day, and we must part. If in the twilight of memory we should meet once more, we shall speak again together and you shall sing to me a sweeter song. And if our hands should meet in another dream we shall build another tower in the sky.

"Kiss me now as I go so that when I awaken on that far shore, I will remember what lulled me so gently to sleep: the touch of your lips on mine."

So saying the Avatar made a signal to the seamen, and straightaway they weighed anchor and cast the ship from its moorings, and they moved eastward. And a cry came from the comrades and friends as from a single heart, and it rose into the dusk and was carried out over the sea like a great chorus.

Only Eva was silent, gazing after the ship until it had vanished into the mist. And when all the people had gone, she stood alone upon the sea-wall, remembering in her heart his saying: "A little while, my darling rosebud, a little while longer; a moment of rest upon the wind, and another woman shall bear me."

171

www.ingramcontent.com/pod-product-compliance
Lightning Source LLC
Chambersburg PA
CBHW080530090426

42733CB00015B/2539

* 9 7 8 1 6 0 6 1 1 1 9 8 7 *